WRITTEN BY
KIM CHAKANETSA

ILLUSTRATED BY
ALABI MAYOWA

WIDE EYED EDITIONS

CONTENTS

4–5 WELCOME TO AFRICA
    6–7 What is Africa?

8–9 AFRICA
    10–11 Out of Africa
    12–13 A Continent of Contrasts

14–15 NORTH AFRICA
    16–17 Dynamic Dynasties
    18–19 People and Cultures of North Africa
    20–21 Wildlife and Landscapes
    22–23 Change Makers and Superstars
    24–25 Snapshots

26–27 EAST AFRICA
    28–29 The Cradle of Humanity
    30–31 People and Culture of East Africa
    32–33 Wildlife and Landscapes
    34–35 Change Makers and Superstars
    36–37 Snapshots

38–39 CENTRAL AFRICA
    40–41 Conquering Kingdoms and Mass Migration
    42–43 People and Cultures of Central Africa
    44–45 Wildlife and Landscapes
    46–47 Change Makers and Superstars
    48–49 Snapshots

50–51 WEST AFRICA
    52–53 Power and Prosperity
    54–55 People and Cultures of West Africa
    56–57 Wildlife and Landscapes
    58–59 Change Makers and Superstars
    60–61 Snapshots

62–63 SOUTHERN AFRICA
    64–65 Great Empires
    66–67 People and Cultures of Southern Africa
    68–69 Wildlife and Landscapes
    70–71 Change Makers and Superstars
    72–73 Snapshots

74–75 GLOBAL AFRICA
    76–77 History of Outward Migration
    78–81 Ten Ways Africa has Influenced the World
    82–83 Changemakers and Superstars
    84–87 Words of Wisdom
    88–89 Fast Flag Facts
    90–91 African Flags

92–93 Glossary

94–95 Index

WELCOME TO AFRICA

Each of the maps featured in this book contains information about a different part of Africa. As we explore Africa and its many fascinating countries, we will be using the African Union map as a guide and their commonly accepted groupings of the five geographic regions that make up North, South, Central, East, and West Africa. Just remember, these maps have been designed to tell a story and aren't drawn to scale. But hopefully they will inspire you to explore this incredible continent and find out all you can about its amazing history.

HOW THIS BOOK WORKS

TIMELINE
Each section begins with a historical timeline of each region. Travel back in time and uncover some of the earliest people to live there—and then step right into the modern day and see how things have changed. It's important to note that many of the dates featured are still being debated by historians today. The dates provided here are the most commonly accepted timeframes.

WILDLIFE AND LANDSCAPES
Africa is home to an enormous diversity of wildlife and landscapes. From dry deserts to lush green rainforests, this section uncovers the rich kaleidoscope of nature and wildlife across this vast continent.

CHANGE MAKERS AND SUPERSTARS
Meet six inspiring people who are part of the rich history and culture of each region of Africa.

PEOPLE AND CULTURE
Africa is a continent full of remarkably diverse communities and cultures all with their own traditions and customs. These spreads feature just a few of the communities and cultures that can be found all over Africa.

SNAPSHOTS
These spreads feature a collection of facts that allow you to discover more about one particular region. From music to protests to renewable resources, discover what makes each region of Africa wonderfully unique!

- -

A NOTE ON DATES
Many African societies kept their records orally instead of in written form. As historians have tended to rely on written records it has meant that there is not always consistency or consensus when it comes to dates in African history.

WHAT IS AFRICA

Get ready to explore Africa—the second largest continent in the world and a place of great contrasts: of bustling mega cities; wide-open savannas; snowy highlands, and scorching deserts. Africa is made up of 54 countries, each with their own unique landscapes, people, and character, and is home to more than 1.3 billion people. Given its size it's no surprise that more than 2,000 languages are spoken there, including Afar, Bemba, Lingala, Shona, Wolof, and Xhosa. That's about 30% of all the world's languages! From the Berbers of North Africa and the Maasai of East Africa to the Yoruba in West Africa and the Herero in Southern Africa, this is a continent of remarkably diverse communities and cultures!

XHOSA is one of South Africa's eleven official languages. It also is one of a few languages around the world which uses click sounds.

THE MOTHER CONTINENT

Scientists and archaeologists have found fossils dating back millions of years that indicate human life began in Africa. Because of this, the continent is sometimes referred to as the "Mother Continent." The continent has a rich and vibrant history spanning millions of years and covering many different civilizations including those of the Ancient Egyptians, the great empires of Songhai, and the Ghana Empire to name a few. As well as its astonishing diversity of peoples, languages, and nations, Africa is also renowned for its rich and varied landscapes and wildlife. Walk through the dense forest of the Virunga Mountains and you may well encounter the mountain gorilla, one of the largest primates in the world. Take a visit to the Serengeti National Park and you might come across a herd of great African elephants striding through the grasslands. Trek up the Ethiopian highlands, home to some of the continent's highest mountains, and if you are lucky, you might spot an Ethiopian wolf. From "Nollywood"—Nigeria's vast film industry—to Kenya's "Silicon Savanna," contemporary Africa is a place of creativity and ingenuity.

AFRICAN ELEPHANTS are the world's largest land animals. Elephant calves are able to stand up within 30 minutes of being born and are able to walk within one or two hours.

MOUNTAIN GORILLAS are one of the most powerful primates. An average male mountain gorilla can weigh 400 pounds.

AFRICA

Africa is a place of stunning natural beauty and hidden treasures.

From its vast deserts and dense rainforests to its vibrant urban skylines—its landscapes are as diverse as its animal kingdoms.

Africa is a place of bold dreamers and bright minds—a continent of unlimited potential!

Across Africa there are many boundary and territorial disputes. Most of them were inherited from colonial powers that created arbitrary borders when they divided the continent among themselves at the Berlin West Africa Conference of 1884–1885. Some of these disputes are minor, like whether a certain country should be grouped with the East Africa region or with Southern Africa. However, others are of a much higher stake. There is a long-running dispute between people living in the Western Sahara and Morocco. At the heart of the conflict was a desire to be an independent territory. But the sparsely populated area on the northwest coast of Africa was annexed by Morocco in 1975, meaning that Morocco took possession of the territory. This led to an enduring conflict which eventually ended in 1991 when the United Nations brokered a peace deal. Despite the truce, the territorial dispute remains unresolved.

The **SAHARA** is the world's largest hot desert.

WESTERN SAHARA

Lake Retba (or Lac Rose) is a famous pink lake in **SENEGAL**. The lake's shade of pink is a result of micro algae in the water.

The people of **GUINEA-BISSAU** are referred to as

ALGERIA is the biggest country in Africa. It covers an area of about 919,000 square miles.

TUNISIA

LIBYA is covered mostly by desert. The Libyan desert itself can go for decades without receiving any rainfall.

The 365-day calendar was invented in **EGYPT** in around 4000 BC.

The longest river in the world is **THE NILE RIVER**. It is 4,100 miles long and flows through 11 countries: Egypt, Eritrea, Sudan, South Sudan, Ethiopia, Uganda, Kenya, Tanzania, Rwanda, Burundi, Democratic Republic of Congo.

Similar to Egypt, **SUDAN** has historical pyramids. There are more than 200 pyramids. The most popular ones are the Meroë Pyramids.

SOUTH SUDAN is the world's newest nation.

ETHIOPIA is the only African country with its own indigenous alphabet.

MOROCCO

MAURITANIA

SENEGAL

GUINEA-BISSAU

GUINEA

Burkina Faso means "land of honest people."

MALI

BURKINA FASO

NIGER

ALGERIA

LIBYA

CHAD

EGYPT

SUDAN

ERITREA

DJIBOUTI

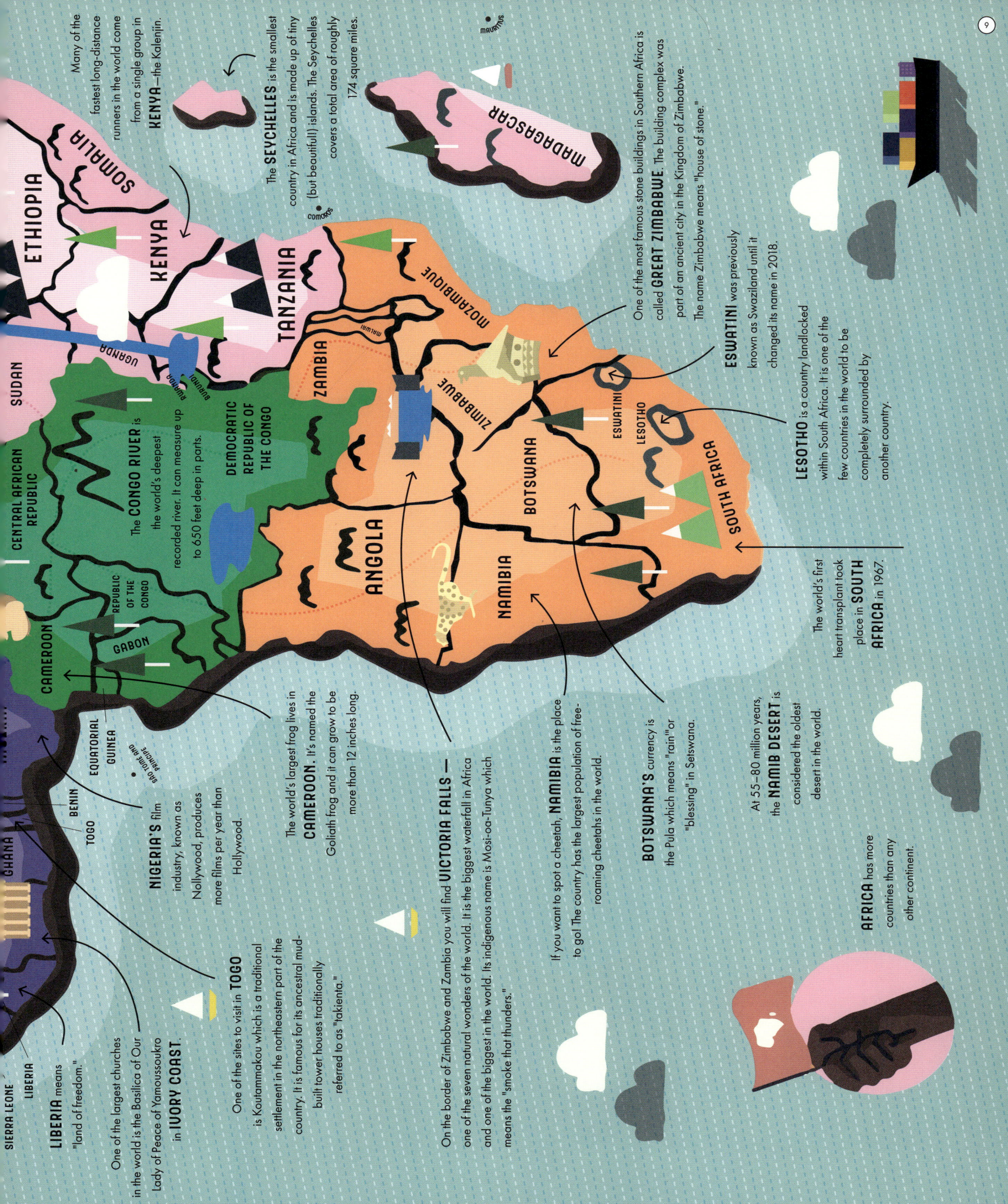

OUT OF AFRICA

We are all a little bit African, as human life started in Africa roughly three million years ago! Scientists have discovered fossilized human remains in East Africa showing where our hominin ancestors first diverged from chimps, began walking upright, started using tools, and ultimately migrated around the world.

BANTU MIGRATION
About 2,000-3,000 years ago, there was a massive migration of people across Africa. Bantu-speaking populations gradually left their original homeland in West-Central Africa and traveled to the eastern and southern regions of Africa. The migration lasted for 1,500 years. It is not clear why Bantu-speaking people left their homes. Today, the Bantu-speaking population is made up of around 310 million people.

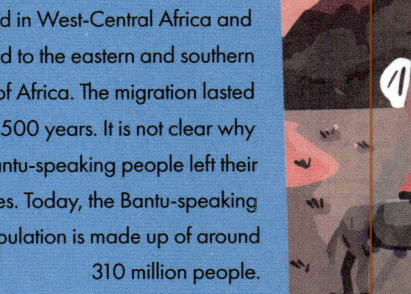

c.3100-332 BC
ANCIENT EGYPT
The Ancient Egyptian civilization began about 5,000 years ago and lasted around 3,000 years. It is famous for its remarkable pyramids, pharaohs, tombs and mummies.

c.1480-1866 AD
THE TRANSATLANTIC SLAVE TRADE
Starting from the 15th century, an era known as the Age of Discovery began. During that time European sailors began exploring the globe looking for goods to trade. Portuguese sailors led the exploration of Africa, but they were quickly followed by other Europeans, such as the British and Spanish. These explorers also sought to obtain and sell commodities such as copper, textiles and ivory. They also were seeking another "commodity": humans. This was the beginning of the slave trade.

c.1100-1450 AD
GREAT ZIMBABWE
The remnants of the capital city of an indigenous empire that thrived between the 11th and 15th centuries can be found in what is now known as Zimbabwe. The ruins of the city are made up of impressive stone towers and defensive walls and are known as Great Zimbabwe. It was one of the first cities in Southern Africa.

THE SLAVE TRADE

An estimated 12 million Africans were taken across the Atlantic to the new colonies in America, South America, and the Caribbean to work in fields, plantations and mines.

While the European slave traders became rich, it was devastating for the slaves who were separated from their families, denied their freedom and treated with great cruelty and violence. Slaves were forced to obey their owners and had to work very long hours in harsh conditions for no pay.

For Europeans, unpaid slave labor helped fund the growth of their empires and paid for the construction of many of the great buildings still seen in European cities today. For the slaves, it damaged the lives of millions of Africans and their descendants. The impact of that dark period of history continues to be felt. Descendants of African slaves in countries like America are still living with the consequences of slavery today.

ETHIOPIA and **LIBERIA** are two countries which were not colonized.

c.1884-1914
THE SCRAMBLE FOR AFRICA
Towards the end of the 19th century the trade of slaves came to an end. During this time European nations were looking to accumulate more wealth and power by invading and seizing African countries (or "colonies," as they called them). The colonizers, those responsible for dividing Africa up, did so without the agreement of the Africans living there. The new borders did not take into account the people, culture, and geography of these places. These changes have remained a source of disagreement and conflict up until today.

c. 100BC–700AD
THE KINGDOM OF AKSUM

The Aksumite Empire was one of the most important trading hubs in northeast Africa. The empire extended across northern Ethiopia through to the Eritrean Highlands and included parts of Sudan and Somalia from the 1st century BC to the 8th century AD. The kingdom is considered one of the four greatest civilizations of the ancient world and is known for a number of achievements such as its own script, known as the Ge'ez alphabet. The Aksum were one of the first civilizations that officially embraced Christianity, in the 4th century.

800BC–1200AD
GHANA EMPIRE

The Ghana Empire, also known as the Wagadou Empire, lies in what is now western Mali, eastern Senegal and southeastern Mauritania. It is one of the great medieval trading empires of western Africa and made its wealth from gold. Despite its name this ancient empire is not related in any way to modern Ghana!

c. 1200–1600AD
THE GREAT EMPIRES OF MALI AND SONGHAI

In Mali, two of the largest empires in African history dominated for 300 years! The first was established in the 13th century under the leadership of Sundiata Keita and the second in the 15th century under Sonni Ali the Great.

c. 500–1500AD
KINGDOM OF IFE

The kingdom of Ife was a powerful West African kingdom that emerged in 500 AD and flourished between 1100 and 1500 AD. Its wealth was partly from its ability to access lucrative trade routes and networks. Ife is renowned for its extraordinary and realistic sculptures made up of bronze, copper and terracotta.

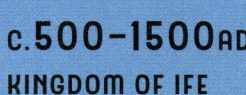

The United Kingdom, France, Germany, Italy, Portugal, Spain and Belgium were all **COLONIAL POWERS**.

c. 1884–1914
THE COLONIAL PERIOD

Over the following 75 years, the colonial powers ruled these countries in different ways. And although they built train tracks and bridges that remain to this day, the colonial system was designed to enrich the Europeans at the expense of the locals. Colonization dramatically changed Africa.

1957
INDEPENDENCE!

On 6 March 1957, Ghana became the first sub-Saharan African country to achieve independence. This meant that the colonial powers were no longer in charge. Kwame Nkrumah was independent Ghana's first leader. Ghana becoming independent was an important moment not just for Ghana but for the continent as a whole and other countries soon followed in its footsteps.

1994
END OF APARTHEID

In April 1994, South Africa's first democratic elections were held that allowed all races to vote. Nelson Mandela was elected as the country's first Black president!

A CONTINENT OF CONTRASTS

Africa is a continent full of character, color and contrasts! If you were to jump into a truck or trek by foot from Cairo in the North to Cape Town in the South you would encounter an astounding range of peoples, cultures, landscapes, wildlife, and plants!

GEOGRAPHY

The Sahara Desert is the world's largest hot desert and the name Sahara means "desert" in Arabic. It covers most of North Africa and is bigger than Brazil! It is said that if the desert were a country, it would be the fifth largest country in the world. But the soaring desert temperatures and sand dunes of the Sahara are in sharp contrast to the green valleys, high mountains and rivers of the Kingdom of Lesotho located in Southern Africa. Lesotho is sometimes referred to as the "Kingdom of the Sky" because the lowest point in the mountainous country is 4,600 feet above sea level. It is considered the highest country in the world and as a result of this elevation Lesotho's climate is cooler than in most other regions at the same latitude.

LESOTHO is one of three nations that is enclaved (completely surrounded) by another country in the world. It is surrounded by South Africa. The others are the Republic of San Marino and the Vatican City, both enclaved within Italy.

Sahara Desert

LIFESTYLE

The Himba of Northern Namibia are known for leading a traditional lifestyle which has remained unchanged for generations. They live a semi-nomadic lifestyle breeding cattle and goats. They are renowned for their striking red matted braids, which they cover with a mixture called otjize as part of their beautification ritual. Otjize is made by mixing butterfat and ground ochre, a stone found locally. Elsewhere, if you walk the streets of Brazzaville (Republic of the Congo) or Kinshasa (Democratic Republic of Congo) you're likely to experience a vastly different way of life. Here you can meet Sapeurs or Sapeuses—flamboyantly dressed men and women known for their love of stylish Western clothes. Their wardrobes of three-piece suits, colorful bow ties, and canes bring together an appreciation of old-school tailoring, but they wear it with a fresh and colorful Congolese flair.

Ndebele home

Lalibela Church

ARCHITECTURE

Across the continent you will find a range of distinct architecture that pays tribute to the long and varied histories and cultures of people. In South Africa, the Ndebele used dung and soil to color their homes, which are known for their bold geometric patterns. The tradition of painting on the house walls dates back to the 18th century and was a way to announce things like family values or marriages.

However, if you travel to the town of Lalibela in Ethiopia you will find a very different style of architecture. Dating back more than 3,000 years are a number of well-preserved churches which span Ethiopia's many kingdoms and dynasties. The Church of St. George or Bete Giorgis is one of the most famous of these medieval churches. It is unique in that it was carved down into the ground out of solid volcanic rock around the 12th century AD. It is an amazing feat of architecture.

FÊTE DU VODOUN, or National Voodoo Day is a public holiday in Benin.

RELIGION

As is to be expected of a continent of many people and cultures, there isn't just one single African religion or belief. People's religious identity is often related to where they are from. Islam and Christianity continue to play a major role but so do local traditional beliefs. In the West African country of Benin, Voodoo is recognised as an official religion. Voodoo is considered to be more than a belief system. It is seen as a way of life, including culture, philosophy, language, art, dance, music, and medicine.

It is also not uncommon for people to mix religious and traditional beliefs. For example, in Zimbabwe a Shona person who is a Christian might adhere to certain traditional customs—they might, for example, call on their Vadzimu or "ancestral spirits" for protection or guidance and observing certain rituals when it comes to births, marriages, and deaths.

ANIMALS

The world's largest land animal makes its home in Africa. The African elephant can grow to be more than ten feet tall and weigh around 13,200 pounds. In contrast, one of the smallest mammals can also be found in Africa! It is related to the elephant but is as tiny as a mouse and measures just 12 inches long! It is called the elephant shrew and has a distinctive trunk-like nose which it uses to feast on insects.

NORTH AFRICA

North Africa is made up of six countries that sit up in the northern part of the continent. These are Algeria, Egypt, Libya, Morocco, Mauritania, and Tunisia. Much like the rest of the continent, North Africa is very diverse in its landscape. Within the region you will find mountains, deserts, grasslands, rivers, and valleys!

The **ATLAS MOUNTAINS** stretch across northwestern Africa and extend for about 1,250 miles through Algeria, Morocco and Tunisia.

TUNISIA is the smallest country in North Africa.

MOROCCO is one of only three kingdoms (a territory ruled by a king or queen) left on the continent of Africa. The others are Lesotho and Eswatini. The University of Al-Karaouine was founded here in 859 and is one of the oldest universities in the world.

WESTERN SAHARA consists mainly of desert and is sparsely populated.

ALGERIA is the largest African country by area (it covers over two million square kilometres). One of the most famous North African sites of rock painting, Tassili n'Ajjer, is located here. It has more than 15,000 rock paintings and engravings, dating back as far as 12,000 years.

In **MAURITANIA**, you can find the "Eye of the Sahara" or the "Eye of Africa." It is a dome-shaped rock structure which stretches about 31 miles across. From space, the structure, which is also called the "Richat Structure," is said to look like a bullseye!

COUSCOUS is a North African staple dish and is it often served alongside meat, fish, stews, and vegetables. Couscous is a grain made from durum wheat semolina.

DYNAMIC DYNASTIES

North Africa is a dynamic region with a rich and impressive history. It was home to one of the greatest and most powerful civilizations: Ancient Egypt. Today it is a vibrant mix of traditional and modern—you'll find nomads herding camels and goats on the fringes of the deserts as well as sprawling mega cities. The region's diversity is reflected in its landscape of mountains, deserts, grasslands, rivers, and valleys.

8000–6000 BC STONE AGE
A DIFFERENT SAHARA

During this period, the Sahara Desert was not the dry and sand-covered place we know today. Back then the vast area received plenty of rainfall and was covered in grassland. It was even inhabited by wildlife such as elephants, rhinos and hippos. A change in weather patterns later transformed it into a barren desert and today it is one of the driest places on earth.

7TH CENTURY
THE ARAB CONQUESTS

The Arab conquest of North Africa began in 640 BC under the leadership of a military ruler known as Amr ibn al-As. He led a 4,000-strong army from Mecca and began capturing and seizing towns. He is regarded as a figure of great historical importance for his role in introducing Islam to the region and the conquests would eventually lead to the establishment of Islam as one of the great religions of the world.

FROM 122 BC
ROMAN INVASION

Over time, Carthage's power and influence spread from North Africa through to Sicily. The Romans perceived it as a threat and this kickstarted the first of three wars which would ultimately lead to Rome destroying the city of Carthage in 146 BC.

The period that stretched between the 7th and 16th centuries was one of constant change and turbulence across the region with different **DYNASTIES** rising and falling. Some of the notable dynasties include the Umayyad dynasty, the Abbasid dynasty, the Fatimid dynasty, and the Ayyubid dynasty of Salah al Din Yusuf ibn Ayyub.

1062–1147 AD
THE ALMORAVIDS DYNASTY

The Almoravid dynasty emerged as a new Islamic power. The Almoravids were ethnically more Berber than Arab, meaning they were a member of the indigenous people of North Africa. In 1062 they conquered Morocco and made Marrakesh the capital. Over time the Almoravids also came to rule parts of the Sahara, Morocco, Algeria and Spain.

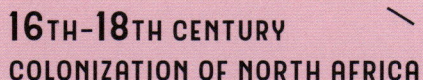

1951–1962
INDEPENDENCE

After World War Two North Africa began claiming its independence. Libya gained independence from Italy in 1951; Tunisia, Morocco, and Algeria underwent a prolonged fight to gain independence from the French, which ended in 1956 when the French granted full independence. Algeria then later gained its independence in 1962.

16TH–18TH CENTURY
COLONIZATION OF NORTH AFRICA

European powers began to see the benefits of claiming territory in Africa and by the end of the 19th century all of North Africa was colonized by various European powers. Italy had cemented rule over Libya, Morocco was a French protectorate, Algeria and Tunisia were under French control and Egypt was a British protectorate.

c. 6000–3000 BC
NEOLITHIC FARMING

Over time there was a move away from hunting and gathering, which had been the primary means of survival. People progressed towards a more settled lifestyle as farming was introduced and animals such as cattle were domesticated.

FROM c. 3000 BC
EGYPTIAN CIVILISATION

The Ancient Egyptian civilization spanned thousands of years, ruled by kings and queens called pharaohs. It is renowned for its highly distinctive culture and numerous achievements, including massive stone pyramids which were built as tombs for their pharaohs. They were a highly religious civilization, worshipped numerous gods and goddesses and believed in the afterlife. When a person of importance died, they would preserve their body through a process of mummification.

800 BC – 689 AD
FOUNDING OF CARTHAGE

A civilization of sea traders from modern day Syria and Lebanon called the Phoenicians raided the Mediterranean coast. They founded the city of Carthage in modern Tunisia. Over time Carthage became the powerful and wealthy capital of the Punic Empire thanks to its impressive network of trade routes.

1130–1269 AD
THE ALMOHADS DYNASTY

The Almoravid dynasty was succeeded by the Almohads who managed to conquer the entire North African coast and unite all Berbers into one singular empire. While maintaining Marrakesh as their centre of power in North Africa, they made Seville their capital in Spain.

1805–1848
VICEROY OF EGYPT

Following centuries of rule under the Ottoman Empire an army officer called Muhammad Ali took power in Egypt. He not only brought about stability but helped to grow the country's economy and influence. He is regarded by some as the father of modern Egypt.

16TH–19TH CENTURY
THE OTTOMAN RULE

Following the decline of the Berber dynasties, all of North Africa, apart from Morocco, fell under Ottoman (Turkish) rule until the 19th century.

PEOPLE AND CULTURES OF NORTH AFRICA

North Africa was historically inhabited by the Berbers along with Tuareg nomads and a few other local groups. Despite centuries of invasions, colonization, and foreign rule, North Africa has managed to retain a distinct identity and a rich cultural heritage. The arrival of Islam in the region as a result of the Arab conquest in the 7th century has had an enduring influence on North Africa's culture, language and religion.

BERBERS

The Berbers, also known as the "Amazigh," are a community of people who have been living in North Africa for centuries and are considered the earliest inhabitants of the region. Up until North Africa was conquered by Arabs, Berbers dominated the region. Today, they can be found in Morocco, Algeria, Libya, and Tunisia as well as in other parts of the continent. Today it is more language and culture that set Berbers apart from other communities and their culture is renowned for its distinctive crafts, dress, and architecture.

The term **"AMAZIGH"** means "free people" in the indigenous Tamazight language.

TUAREG

The Tuareg are a nomadic people descended from the Berbers of North Africa and have been largely Muslim since the 16th century. They share their own language called Tamasheq and are sometimes called the "blue men of the Sahara" because of their trademark indigo gowns. They are known for their traveling camel caravans across the desert.

EGYPTIANS

The term Egyptian refers to both an ethnic group and a nationality. Egypt was home to one of the world's earliest civilizations and has an incredible history of language and culture. Egyptian was one of the first written languages in the world, in the form of hieroglyphics.

BEDOUINS

The Bedouin (meaning "desert dwellers" in Arabic) are a group of people who originated in the Arabian Peninsula and spread across Northern Africa. Some Bedouin people live in tents, moving from place to place herding cattle and goats. However, since the middle of the 20th century, many have settled in cities, adopting a modern lifestyle.

COPTS

Coptic Christians or Copts are an ethnic religious group indigenous to North Africa. The majority of Copts live in Egypt but they can also be found in Sudan and Libya. Copts have their own pope and follow a different calendar to the rest of the Christian world. The Church separated from other Christian denominations in 451 AD after a disagreement about the human and divine nature of Jesus Christ. The early Coptic Church suffered persecution under the Roman Empire and faced intermittent persecutions after Egypt became a Muslim country Many believe that these persecutions still continue today.

SEPHARDI AND MIZRAHI JEWS

Before widescale emigration in the early 1960s, North Africa's Jewish communities were among the largest in the world. Mizrahi Jews were indigenous to North Africa; the earliest among them predate the arrival of Islam. Sephardic Jews were refugees from Portugal and Spain in the Renaissance era.

MAGHREB, NILE VALLEY AND SAHEL

The ethnic groups living in North Africa are divided by the geographical regions of Maghreb, Nile valley, and Sahel (Sahara).

The **NILE VALLEY** and delta are home to the majority of Egyptians.

Historically known as the Barbary coast, a name derived from the Berbers, who were the region's main inhabitants, **THE MAGHREB** includes the countries of Algeria, Libya, Morocco, and Tunisia. In the Maghreb region, Berbers are the majority and the Berber language is spoken by 60% of the population. Due to conquests in the ancient times, the region is also home to ethnic Arabs, French, Sephardic Jews, and West Africans.

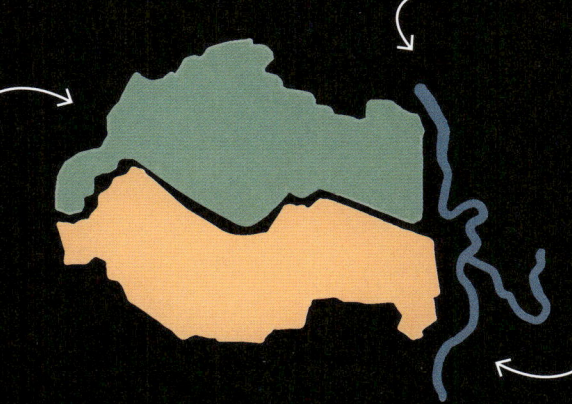

THE SAHEL is the region between the Sahara Desert to the north and the Sudanian savanna in the south and has a semi-arid climate. Sahel in Arabic means "coast" or "shore." Most people of the Sahel were traditionally semi-nomads mainly farming and raising livestock.

WILDLIFE AND LANDSCAPES

North Africa is home to stunning landscapes and areas of impressive biodiversity. It has four main geographic regions, each home to an incredible collection of creatures big and small.

Africa's largest crocodile can be found in the Nile. The **NILE CROCODILE** is an aggressive predator with a fearsome reputation thanks to its long powerful jaw, quick reflexes and speed. The male Nile crocodile can grow up to twenty feet long!

THE NILE VALLEY AND DESERT

The Nile delta and valley are formed by the River Nile that flows through Egypt. The Nile River flows from south to north, through eastern Africa and is one of the longest rivers in the world. The Nile River was critical to the development of ancient Egypt. The fertile soil was ideal for growing crops such as wheat, barley, and papyrus. In Ancient Egypt the papyrus plant was used to make cloth, rope, and paper. Much of Egypt's food has been cultivated in the Nile delta region and, even today, the Nile River continues to be an important trade route and a convenient mode of transport not just for Egyptians but for people living in the Nile River Basin countries, such as Uganda.

ADDAX are a part of the antelope family that tend to congregate in the Sahara. They are perfectly suited to desert life as they need very little water to survive. Addax are about one metre tall and hunt in packs at night.

Also found in the Sahara is the **DAMA GAZELLE** and with its dark red coat and white underbelly, it is one of the most striking animals in North Africa. They can live alone or in herds and mainly feed off plants and trees.

CENTRAL SAHARA

The Central Sahara is an incredibly arid place with little to no vegetation growing there. It has several distinct physical features that are well-known for features such as rocky stone plateaus, ergs, or sand seas which are large areas covered with sand dunes. The desert features are shaped by wind or rainfall to form sand dunes, dry valleys (wadi), dry lakes (oued), salt flats, and gravel plains (reg). The Sahara serves as a geographical boundary between North Africa and sub-Saharan Africa.

ATLAS MOUNTAINS

The Atlas Mountains run from east to west of North Africa. The mountain ranges stretch parallel to the Mediterranean coast, separating the Mediterranean Sea from the Sahara.

The Atlas range is home to different plants and animals that are completely unique to Africa. It also has some fascinating wildlife. The barbary ape is mostly found in the Algerian and Moroccan Atlas mountains. It is known for its unusual parenting where the males mostly raise all the infant monkeys.

MEDITERRANEAN COAST

The Mediterranean coast is the strip of coastal area where the Mediterranean Sea meets the land. The coast was once home to herds of mammals, but they have diminished in numbers with the drying of the Sahara.

Most of the wildlife in the Mediterranean region is found in the woodlands and forests. The **BARBARY STAG**, which is also known as the Atlas deer, is a subspecies of red deer found in North Africa (mainly in Morocco, Algeria and Tunisia) and is the only deer known to be native to Africa. It is dark brown with white spots on its flanks and back and is happiest living in dense, humid forest areas.

HYENAS also roam the Mediterranean coast. These wild creatures look like large dogs with long faces and slightly skinny bodies. They are nomadic and tend to hunt alone rather than in packs. They're mostly found in savannas, woodlands, and grasslands. The chances of spotting a striped hyena in this part of the world used to be very high but sadly, due to habitat loss and hunting, the hyena is now under threat.

CHANGE MAKERS AND SUPERSTARS

MOHAMED SALAH (B.1992)

Mohamed Salah is an Egyptian footballer who plays as a forward for Premier League club Liverpool and is also the captain of Egypt's National Team. Mohamed or "Mo" is known for his dazzling skills on the pitch and his generosity and modest manner off the pitch. Travel through Cairo and beyond and you won't fail to see Mo's face, which is on everything from bed linen to billboards paying tribute to Egypt's hometown hero! He is considered one of football's top players.

NAWAL EL SAADAWI (1931-2021)

Nawal El Saadawi was an Egyptian author of more than 55 books, activist, physician, and trailblazer who built a reputation as a fearless and tireless advocate for women's rights. Throughout her life Nawal defended the rights of women against social and religious constraints and fought for change.

NAGUIB MAHFOUZ (1911-2006)

The Egyptian author Naguib Mahfouz is considered one of the greatest Arab novelists of the 20th century. A prolific writer, he has produced more than 30 books and in 1988, he became the first Arab to win the Nobel Prize for Literature. Much of his work has been turned into television dramas and films. His novels centred on the lives of ordinary Egyptians in Cairo.

AHMED H. ZEWAIL (1946-2016)

In 1999, Ahmed H. Zewail won the Nobel Prize in Chemistry and in doing so became the first Arab to win a Nobel in any of the sciences. His award was related to a revolutionary technique he had developed to study chemical reactions in detail. He was also credited for championing science education and research in Egypt and the Middle East.

HISHAM MATAR (B.1970)

Hisham Matar is an award-winning Libyan-British novelist. In 2017, he accepted the prestigious Pulitzer Prize in Biography for his memoir, *The Return*. The book describes Matar's journey back to his native Libya in 2012 to search for the truth about the disappearance of his father, a prominent political figure.

HASSAN HAJJAJ (B.1961)

Hassan Hajjaj is a Moroccan artist renowned for his colorful work which is heavily influenced by pop art, hip hop, fashion, and his North African heritage. Hajjaj often uses photography, film, and printed fabric to represent his playful and vibrant ideas.

SNAPSHOTS

MUSICAL FLAVOURS

North Africa is home to a vibrant and evolving music scene. Each country offers a different flavour and flair. Algeria is the birthplace of the rebellious Algerian pop called Raï whose roots are in traditional folklore. Since its emergence in the 1920s, Raï has evolved to incorporate different influences such as flamenco, French chanson (traditional song), jazz, and other styles into its mix.

Gnawa is another type of music which dates back to the 12th century. It is played on a three-stringed instrument called the guembri. Gnawa is the music of formerly enslaved Black Africans who came to Morocco from sub-Saharan countries, and preserves the traditions and folkloric music of their ancestors. For a long time, women were not allowed to play Gnawa but that is changing and young female artists like Asmaa Hamzaoui are shaking things up. Asmaa was the first female guembri player in Morocco.

In Mauritania, rap has emerged as the music of protest with artists tackling topics that affect their daily lives including racism, poverty, and inequality. While in Morocco, "nayda" is a youth movement of a new wave of artists and musicians who are taking their cues from their local heritage and singing words of freedom and protest in the Moroccan-Arabic dialect of darija.

FANCY A FESTIVAL?

Whether it is desert rock, smooth jazz, or funky pop, Morocco has become one of the leading destinations for music festivals. The festival of Mawazine, which means "rhythms of the world" is the second largest festival in the world. Approximately 2.5 million people descend on Rabat, the city where it is held, annually to watch performances by local and international artists. Other musical festivals in Morocco include Jazzablanca in Casablanca, the Gnaoua festival, Timitar, and the Fes Festival. Among the bands that have appeared on stage are Tinariwen, a group of Tuareg musicians from northern Mali and Guinean musician Moh! Kouyaté.

GREEN ALGERIA

Algeria is becoming a green energy leader in the world by investing in natural resources and renewable energy with a target of generating over 27% of electricity from renewable sources by 2030. There are currently plans to build several solar plants. The country's high sun radiation level makes it one of the largest markets for solar power on the continent. In 2014, the country's first wind farm was created and there are further plans to develop the wind power industry.

A NEW CAPITAL

Egypt will soon have a new capital city! It will be located in the desert east of the current capital, Cairo. The city is yet to be officially named and is currently known as the New Administrative Capital. The city will be home to a variety of skyscrapers, one of which is set to be the tallest building in Africa. The new capital will help ease congestion in Cairo and address the current housing shortage.

THE ARAB SPRING

In late 2010, a series of protests started in Tunisia and spread across to Egypt, Libya, and other parts of the Middle East. The uprisings known as the Arab Spring were sparked by a 26-year-old Tunisian man called Mohamed Bouazizi who had grown frustrated by state corruption and police brutality. The protests that followed eventually brought down Tunisia's long-term leader Zine El Abidine Ben Ali. The change in leadership ushered in the promise of a more open and democratic society.

EAST AFRICA

From the fascinating history of Africa's oldest independent country, Ethiopia, and the cutting-edge buzz of Kenya's technology hub, known as the Silicon Savannah, to the eye-popping inventiveness of Uganda's filmmakers and Rwanda's vibrant art scene, East Africa is a region fizzing with character, creativity and contradictions.

ERITREA is home to the Danakil depression, one of the lowest and hottest places on earth. Here, temperatures soar to a sweltering 120 degrees Fahrenheit. The landscape is dotted with salt mountains, acid pools and hot springs of smelly sulphur.

Eritrea is located in a region known as the Horn of Africa. The region includes the countries of Djibouti, Eritrea, Ethiopia, and Somalia. The name comes from the horn-shaped land formation that makes up this area.

Lac Assal in **DJIBOUTI** is one of the saltiest lakes in the world, second only to the Don Juan Pond in Antarctica. However, it is not the best place for a swim as the salt would sting a person's skin and leave them feeling very itchy. The salt is, however, useful for trade. Locals dig the salt from the shore and transport it to Ethiopia where it is sold or exchanged for coffee or coal.

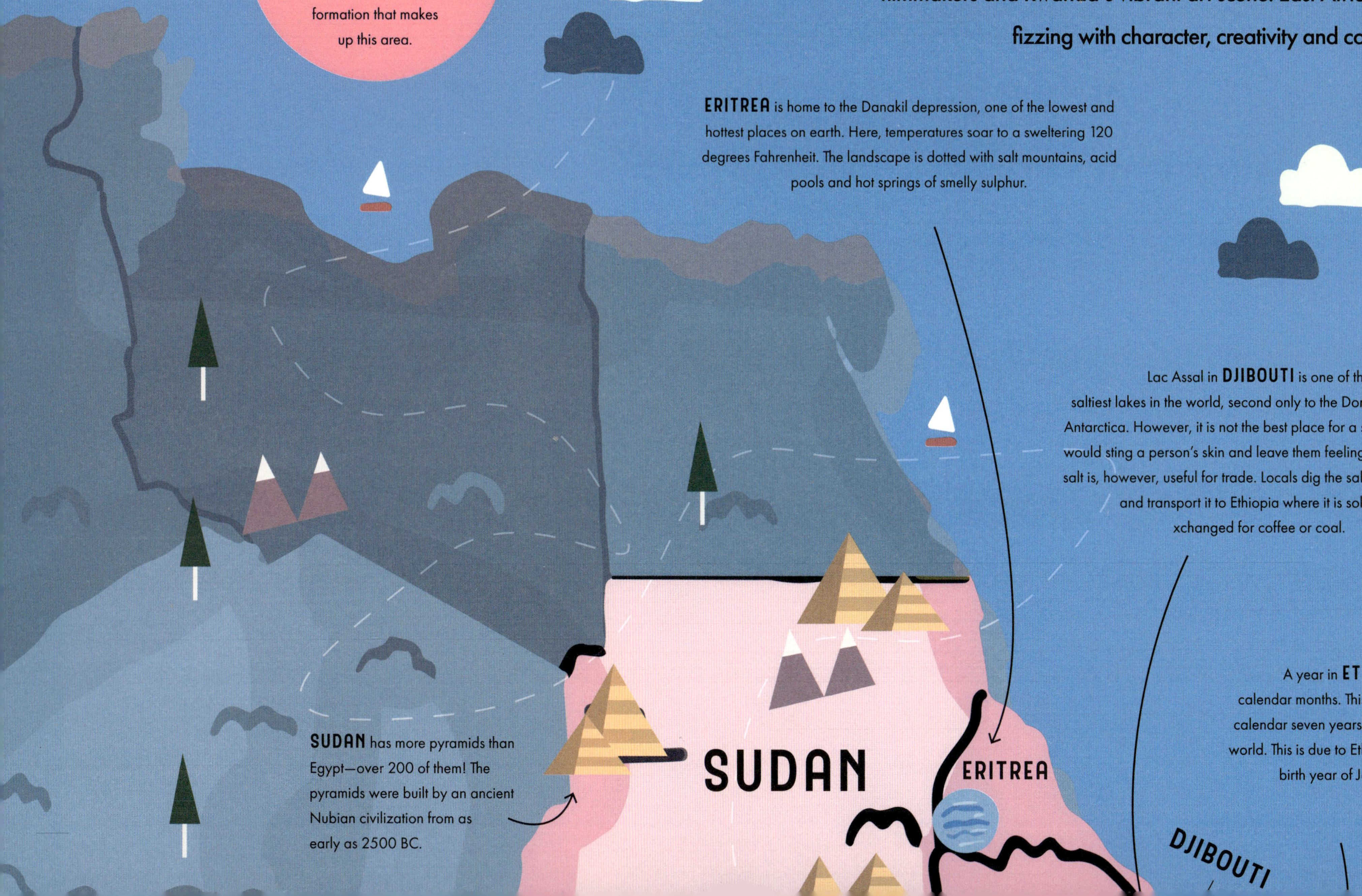

A year in **ETHIOPIA** contains 13 calendar months. This makes the Ethiopian calendar seven years behind the rest of the world. This is due to Ethiopia calculating the birth year of Jesus Christ differently.

SUDAN has more pyramids than Egypt—over 200 of them! The pyramids were built by an ancient Nubian civilization from as early as 2500 BC.

DJIBOUTI

ERITREA

SUDAN

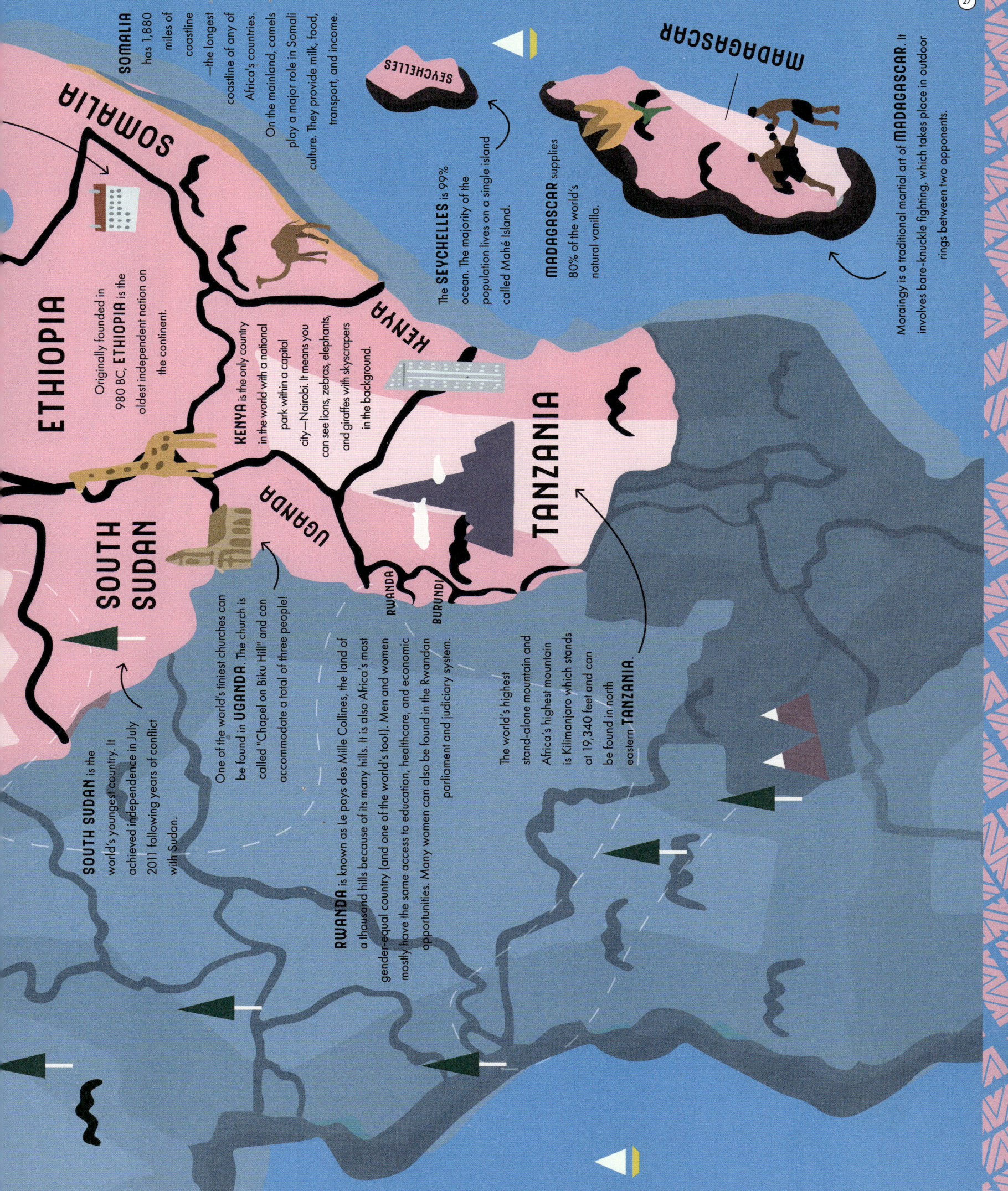

THE CRADLE OF HUMANITY

The earliest human ancestors are estimated to have appeared in East Africa's Rift Valley around 200,000 years ago. Over centuries, the region has been home to impressive empires and kingdoms, including the Kingdom of Aksum in Ethiopia, which is considered one of the greatest empires of its time. With several commercial ports dotted along the East African coast, the region turned into a powerful trading hub. The area's vibrant histories and fascinating stories can be seen still in the traditions, culture, and artefacts of the people today.

c.1500BC–300AD
THE KINGDOM OF KUSH

The Kingdom of Kush is located in what is now Sudan, south of Egypt. The region was called Ta-Seti, meaning "Land of the Bow," which was a nod to the excellent archery skills of its Nubian inhabitants. Access to an abundance of natural resources like gold, ivory, and iron ensured the kingdom's wealth and influence. The Kushites ruled for hundreds of years and in the 8th century BC they managed to conquer and then govern Egypt for nearly 100 years. As a result, the two areas shared cultural, economic and religious links.

1375–PRESENT
THE BUGANDA KINGDOM

The Kingdom of Buganda is one of the oldest traditional kingdoms in East Africa, with a history that dates back some 1,000 years. It was established after a leader known as Kato Kintu conquered the area and began to expand the kingdom eventually turning it into one of the most powerful states in East Africa by the 19th century. This was partly due to the kingdom gaining control of the salt trade over an area known as the Bunyoro, a rival ancient kingdom in the region of the Great Lakes in eastern Africa. In 1966, after a powerful struggle, the kingdom was abolished by Milton Obote, the Prime Minister at the time. The kingdom was later re-established in 1993 and remains an important part of modern-day Uganda. The Buganda kingdom still has a king but the role is largely ceremonial.

c.800AD–1800
KILWA KISIWANI

Another notable East African empire was Kilwa Kisiwani, meaning "isle of the fish." Located off the coast of Tanzania, the island became a wealthy trading port which stretched from Kenya to Mozambique. With access to excellent trading routes, the island was able to export spices and tortoiseshell. Traders from India, China, and parts of Africa also brought their goods to the port. The architectural remnants of this great kingdom can still be seen today. Perhaps most notable is the Great Mosque, which is one of the oldest standing mosques on the East Africa coast.

RWANDAN GENOCIDE

Between April and June 1994, nearly one million people were violently killed in Rwanda. This dark period of history can be traced back to the stoking of ethnic divisions between the Hutus and the Tutsis during Belgian rule. The colonial power seeded the myth that the minority Tutsi were the superior ethnicity. Over time, clashes would occur in which the Tutsis would be attacked by the majority Hutus. This eventually led to the genocide of 1994 in which Tutsi were systematically targeted and killed.

9 JULY 2011
A NEW COUNTRY

South Sudan gained independence from Sudan, ending a long civil war and creating the world's newest country.

1ST–8TH CENTURY AD
THE KINGDOM OF AKSUM

The kingdom of Aksum was located in the Horn of Africa, in what is now the Tigray region of northern Ethiopia. At the heart of the kingdom was the port city of Adulis—a thriving trading hub. Traders from Egypt, India, China, and the Middle East would come to buy salt, ivory, emeralds, and animals—and they, in turn, would sell their iron, glassware, weapons, and wine. The legacy of this powerful ancient kingdom can be seen today in the remaining Aksum monuments, architecture, and in the specially minted Askum coins that were created in gold, silver, and bronze. Askum also had its own script called Ge'ez, which is still in use in Ethiopia today.

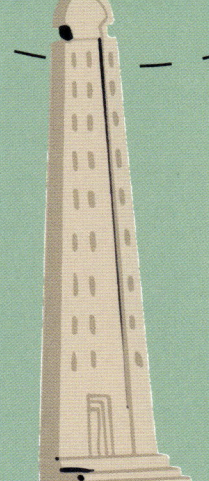

In the 4th century, as **CHRISTIANITY** was spread from North to East Africa by traders and travelers, Aksum became one of the first sub-Saharan states to adopt the religion. The arrival of Arab traders in the coastal areas of East Africa and on the island of Zanzibar saw the growth of **ISLAM**, which then reached other regions in East Africa between the 8th and 10th centuries.

C.1137–1974 AD
ABYSSINIA EMPIRE

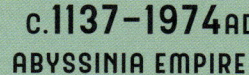

The Ethiopian Empire, also known as Abyssinia, is one of the longest-running empires of all time which was ruled by Zagwe royalty for about 150 years. It was established in what is now modern-day Ethiopia and Eritrea. Between 1200 and 1250 AD, stunning churches were carved out of rock in these regions. They became alternative pilgrimage sites for Christians, whose routes to Jerusalem had been been stopped after the Muslim conquests. These churches are considered some of the most ancient places of worship for Christians. From 1270 AD onwards, the Solomonic dynasty overthrew the Zagwe dynasty as rulers. During this time, the empire conquered virtually all the people within modern Ethiopia. The empire also fought off various foreign armies, including the Italians, Arabs, and Turkish to maintain independence, which they kept for hundreds of years. The Solomonic dynasty continued to rule until 1974, when the last emperor, Haile Selassie, was deposed.

1952–1960
THE MAU MAU UPRISING

By the end of the 19th century much of Africa was under colonial rule. In Kenya, members of the Kikuyu community, who had lost land to white settlers, began an armed campaign against inequality and injustice. The fighters were known as the Mau Mau. Although the uprising was ultimately quashed, the rebellion helped to bring about Kenya's independence in 1963. Numerous other countries within the region also sought and gained independence from colonial rule.

1968
AN IMPORTANT DISCOVERY

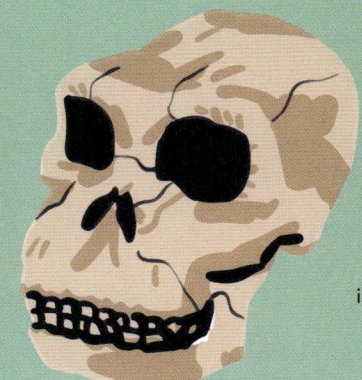

In 1968, a man called Peter Nzube discovered a 1.8-million-year-old Homo habilis (meaning "handy man") skull in Olduvai Gorge in Tanzania. This and other findings at the gorge helped to confirm that the first humans evolved in Africa. The area remains one of the most important fossil sites in the world.

MARCH 2007
MOBILE MONEY REVOLUTION

A money transfer system called M-Pesa was launched in Kenya. It enabled money to be transferred using a basic mobile phone. The system quickly expanded to other countries and became a critical part of Africa's economy, helping people to pay bills, receive salaries and buy insurance. M-Pesa's success sheds light on the promise and potential of Africa's fast-growing financial technology firms.

OCTOBER 2004
A HISTORIC WIN

The Kenyan ecologist and activist Wangari Maathai made history by becoming the first African woman to win the Nobel Peace Prize for her work towards human rights and environmental conservation.

PEOPLE AND CULTURES OF EAST AFRICA

East Africa is a vibrant mix of people, cultures, and languages. Although East African countries have much in common, there are also numerous distinct differences between them. One common factor is the Swahili language, which is spoken widely across the region including Tanzania, Kenya, and Uganda, as well as by some groups in Somalia and Rwanda. Another common factor is religion, with Islam and Christianity being the dominant religions. In parts of Tanzania, Somalia, the horn of Africa and in Eastern Kenya Islam is practiced. Christianity is the dominant religion in the remainder of the region. As in other parts of Africa, traditional African spiritual and religious practices are sometimes also observed alongside Islam and Christianity.

The Tallest: The Dinka

In South Sudan, the Dinka people make up the majority of the population and are famous for their towering height. Some Dinka men stand at a dizzying height of 7 foot tall. It is unclear why some Dinka people grow to such an incredible height but this physical attribute can really come in handy. Take Manute Bol, for example. He is a South Sudanese basketball player who joined the National Basketball Association (NBA) in 1985. At around 7 foot and 7 inches, he was one of the tallest NBA players ever and stood way above his teammates and rivals!

The Fastest: The Kalenjin

Kenyans have a reputation for being record-beating long-distance runners, and most of these athletes come from the same Kenyan community, the Kalenjin. At the Olympics and Athletics World Championships the Kenyan runners are the ones to watch, with their tendency to constantly sweep the medal table in the 5,000-metre, 10,000-metre and marathon distances. By 2019, Kalenjin athletes had won close to 73% of all of Kenya's gold medals! Scientists have conducted studies to try and understand this phenomenon, with some attributing it to the high altitude in which they train, their genes, and even their diet.

The toughest: The Afar

Imagine living in a place of intense heat, droughts, and volcanoes. For centuries the Afar of Djibouti have lived in a hostile environment north of the rift valley where they mine salt to earn a living. The Afar are a cross-border community, which can be found in Ethiopia and Eritrea, where they live as shepherds, herding livestock. The Afar men are renowned for their distinctive hairstyles of either thick afros or long curls. They often cover their hair in butter to protect it from the sun. The men regularly dress in a cotton toga and carry a curved dagger on their belt known as a jile, which is mainly worn as an accessory but can also be used for fighting.

The nature lovers: The Maasai

Across Kenya and Northern Tanzania is an ethnic group that lives in close connection to nature. For centuries, the Maasai have lived alongside lions, leopards, elephants, and wildebeest. The Maasai's lifestyle centres around cattle. They walk long distances with their livestock in search of pasture. The Maasai are known for their distinctive dress, including a Maasai blanket or red shuka cloth which helps them to endure harsh weather. The Maasai have distinct customs such as the traditional leaping dance known as the adamu. The dance involves Maasai men competing to see who jumps the highest—whoever succeeds can then choose who will be his wife.

WILDLIFE AND LANDSCAPES

East Africa is home to some of Africa's most striking and amazing wildlife and landscapes. Here you will encounter breathtaking landscapes from the snow-capped mountain peaks of Mount Kilimanjaro to the vast grassy plains known as the Serengeti. The region is also home to many of the world's most fascinating animals from the impressive mountain gorilla, which can be found in Rwanda and Uganda, to the extremely rare black leopard, which was last spotted in Kenya in 2019.

THE SERENGETI

The Serengeti National Park is a vast protected ecosystem that spans 12,000 square miles. It stretches from north Tanzania and extends to southwestern Kenya. Made up of woodlands, swamps, riverbank forests, and vast plains it is home to a huge number of cheetahs, elephants, wildebeest, lions, zebras, and giraffes. The Serengeti is most famous for being the site of the largest animal migration on the planet! More than 1.5 million wildebeest, 300,000 gazelle and 200,000 zebras cross the plains and woodlands from northern Tanzania to the Maasai Mara in Kenya and back again in search of food and water. The animals travel over 500 miles or more during each cycle.

THE EAST AFRICAN RIFT VALLEY

Running for thousands of miles in East Africa is a deep trench which was caused by a split in the earth's crust about 35 million years ago. There are two arms to the rift valley—the Eastern and Western. The valley is a vast plain where you will also find some of Africa's highest mountains and deepest lakes. The unique biodiversity of the region can be seen in places like Lake Nakuru, a shallow lake known for its fuchsia flamingos. The elegant pink birds are so numerous it is sometimes called "the pink lake."

THE ETHIOPIAN HIGHLANDS

Most of Africa's highest mountains can be found in the Ethiopian highlands. A place of great beauty, the mountains stretch into Eritrea where they are referred to as the Eritrea Highlands. The area hosts animals, such as the gelada baboon and the endangered Ethiopian wolf, that can't be found anywhere else in the world. Unusual birdlife can also be found in the highlands—species such as the Ethiopian siskin, the Abyssinian catbird, and the Ethiopian bushcrow can all be spotted there.

DISCOVERING LUCY

The Lower Awash Valley in Ethiopia has been instrumental in shaping our understanding of our ancestors. Numerous remains have been found at the site dating back some four million years. In 1974, a team of scientists made one of the most famous discoveries in the area when they came across the roughly 3.2-million-year-old bones belonging to one of our human ancestors who walked upright on two feet. The skeleton, who is named Lucy, is one of the oldest pieces of evidence of our human ancestors.

THE RAINBOW DUNES OF MAURITIUS

Imagine a group of dunes not in the usual sandy brown color but rather in multiple hues: yellow, green, red, purple, blue, violet. These colorful marvels are known as the Seven Colored Earths and can be found in Chamarel, Mauritius. The array of colors are said to be as a result of volcanic activity.

CHANGE MAKERS AND SUPERSTARS

WANGARI MAATHAI (1940-2011)

In 1977, Wangari Maathai founded the Green Belt Movement helping women to plant trees and care for the land. She helped plant more than 50 million trees. An outspoken ecologist and human rights champion, Wangari was a pioneer in many ways. She was the first female professor in Kenya and the first African woman to receive a Nobel Peace Prize in 2004 for her work on peace, sustainable development and democracy.

WINNIE BYANYIMA (B.1959)

Winnie Byanyima is a true trailblazer who has worn many hats in her long career. She was Uganda's first aeronautical engineer and later became involved in local politics and was elected as a member of Uganda's parliament. A champion of women's rights, Winnie has held numerous roles in high-profile organisations, including leading the charity Oxfam International and UNAIDS (The Joint United Nations Programme on HIV/AIDS).

HAILE SELASSIE (1892-1975)

From 1930 to 1974, Haile Selassie reigned as Ethiopia's last Emperor. His full title was "His Imperial Majesty Haile Selassie I, Conquering Lion of the Tribe of Judah, King of Kings and Elect of God." During his decades-long rule the Emperor was viewed as an advocate for African unity and a modernising leader. In 1963, he was the first chairperson of the Organisation of African Unity, the precursor to the African Union. He was even considered by members of the Rastafarian community of Jamaica to be a God. His reign, however, was not without controversy, with some critics arguing about his strong grip on power. His legacy continues in songs by artists such as the Jamaican musician Bob Marley and the Ethiopian singer Teddy Afro.

HAILE GEBRSELASSIE (B.1973)

Growing up on a farm, Haile Gebrselassie had to run long distances to get to school every day (12.5 miles in total). When he later became one of the world's greatest long-distance runners, breaking world records and winning medals, he did so with his left arm crooked as a result of the years he spent running with his school books under his arm.

IMAN ABDULMAJID (B.1955)

Iman was born Zara Mohamed Abdulmajid in Somalia's capital Mogadishu. When a photographer spotted her on the street and asked whether he could take her photo, Iman was hesitant but eventually agreed. That photo would help launch a long and lucrative global modeling career. Iman went on to model and appear on some of the world's most famous catwalks and magazine covers. She is also a cosmetics entrepreneur and, in 1994, she launched a cosmetics brands that catered to Black skin tones.

ABDULRAZAK GURNAH (B.1948)

In October 2021, Tanzanian-British novelist Abdulrazak Gurnah won the 2021 Nobel Prize in Literature for his writing on colonialism and the fate of refugees. The prize is widely seen as the world's most prestigious literary award. Abdulrazak has written ten novels in total and numerous short stories. His work focuses on stories of migration, displacement and dislocation.

SNAPSHOTS

FAST-GROWING ECONOMIES

Three of the most rapidly growing economies can be found in East Africa: Ethiopia, Tanzania, and Rwanda. The strong economic growth is tied to the countries diversifying their industries, so they aren't just reliant on one single industry but many different ones, including fishing tourism, financial services, and manufacturing.

LIGHTS! CAMERA! ACTION!

Just outside of Uganda's capital Kampala is a place called Wakaliga which is now home to a booming and innovative film industry. Called "Wakaliwood," it is Uganda's very own Hollywood. Started by a self-taught filmmaker Isaac Nabwana in 2005, "Wakaliwood" has created over 40 films on tiny budgets using everyday household items such as toilet paper, glue, frying pans, and pipes to create special effects and make-up. One of the most popular films is called *Who Killed Captain Alex?* Uganda's first action movie, which was made with a budget of under $180.

THE SILICON SAVANNAH

The next big world-changing technology invention could come out of Kenya's Silicon Savannah. Kenya's capital Nairobi is home to many technology start-ups that work to solve everyday problems through technology innovations. The name "Silicon Savannah" is a reference to the American technology hub Silicon Valley in California.

CITY OF THE FUTURE

Building on Kenya's reputation as a place of tech innovation, the Kenyan government is developing Konza Technology City, a 5,000-acre technology hub. When completed, this future African city will be home to several IT companies and a new university. Construction is currently underway using "greener" building materials and focusing on sustainable construction. The hope is that the city will also create thousands of jobs.

GOING MOBILE

Africa is the global leader in mobile money and in countries like Tanzania and Kenya mobile money is an essential part of everyday life, enabling people to transfer money via their mobile phones. The beauty of this service is that you don't need to have a bank account or a fancy mobile phone in order to move your money. In Africa today, there are 100 million active mobile money accounts—far more than in any other country.

COFFEE TIME

Did you know that Ethiopia is known as the birthplace of coffee? Ethiopia began exporting coffee in the 17th century and grew the industry in the 19th century. Today, Ethiopia is the largest coffee producer in Africa, exporting millions of coffee bags each year.

CENTRAL AFRICA

The countries that make up the region of Central Africa are all wonderfully unique in character but also share many similarities. The region spans a vast area all around the equator—here you can experience the warm humidity of a tropical rainforest in the Congo, while further north in Chad, you'll uncover the dry heat of the Sahara Desert. It is a landscape of towering mountain ranges, dense green jungles and modern bustling cities.

Africa has the youngest population in the world with almost 60% of the people living there under the age of 25.

The country is named after Lake Chad, which is located on its western border. The word "tsade" means "lake" or "large body of water" in

CHAD

The Bamum script was introduced in the Kingdom of Bamum in 1896 by the ruler, Sultan Ibrahim Njoya. The writing system was initially made up of pictographs then later evolved to include characters representing syllables. Although the script is no longer as widely used today, there is a push to ensure people continue to learn to read and write it to help keep this unique writing system alive.

The **CENTRAL AFRICAN REPUBLIC** is home to nearly 600 species of butterflies of all different shapes, sizes and colors! A species known as the *Papilio antimachus* is found there. It has distinct orange-brown wings with black streaks which can reach up to 10 inches, making it one of the largest butterflies in the world.

In **BURUNDI** cows are a symbol of happiness and prosperity. This is reflected in the Kirundi greeting "amashyo," which translates to "may you have many herds of cattle." The response to this is "amashongore," which means "may you have many herds of female cattle." Kirundu is one of Burundi's official languages.

In 1998 the Katanda harpoon was discovered in Katanda, a region in the northeast of the country. This indicated to historians that the area now known as the **DRC** was populated as early as 90,000 years ago.

BURUNDI

CENTRAL AFRICAN REPUBLIC

DEMOCRATIC REPUBLIC OF THE CONGO

REPUBLIC OF THE CONGO

CAMEROON

GABON

EQUATORIAL GUINEA

São Tomé and Príncipe

There are over 270 languages and dialects spoken across **CAMEROON**!

EQUATORIAL GUINEA got its name because it is near the equator and the Gulf of Guinea.

The twin islands **SÃO TOMÉ AND PRÍNCIPE** were once the world's largest producers of cocoa, which earned them the nickname "the chocolate islands." Ivory Coast and Ghana are now two of the greatest cocoa producers.

Almost 90% of **GABON** is covered by forest. The country is home to more than half of Africa's forest elephants, which are smaller than the savanna elephant. They have straight tusks that point downwards and rounded ears.

The **REPUBLIC OF THE CONGO** is often referred to as Congo (Brazzaville). This is to help distinguish it from its eastern neighbor, the Democratic Republic of Congo, which people tend to refer as the DRC. The Republic of Congo is named after the Kongo kingdom that was located in present day Democratic Republic of Congo and Angola.

CONQUERING KINGDOMS AND MASS MIGRATION

Central African hunter-gatherers belong to one of the oldest lineages of modern humans in the world. Their roots date back as far as 250,000 years ago. The area was then populated by Bantu groups migrating south from West Africa.

10TH CENTURY
RED GOLD
Copper played a big role in the economy in Central Africa. It was used as currency and at one stage was more valuable than gold! Archaeological excavations indicate that copper production in Central Africa dates back to as early as the 10th century. Evidence of extraction and production was found in the south of Congo-Brazzaville that begun at least a thousand years ago.

THE BANTU MIGRATION
About 2000-3000 years ago, there was a massive migration of people across Africa. Bantu-speaking populations gradually left their original homeland in West-Central Africa and traveled to the eastern and southern regions of Africa. The migration lasted for 1,500 years. By 500 BC, some groups had reached the Central African rainforest and absorbed or displaced the indigenous population.

c.1500-1890
THE KINGDOM OF BURUNDI
The Kingdom of Burundi was formed in the 1500s. It was ruled by kings who were referred to as "mwami," meaning "ruler." Beneath the king sat several princes who were in charge of smaller regions. In 1890, Germany colonized Burundi, marking the end of the kingdom.

c.1600-1900
THE KINGDOM OF LUNDA
From the early 17th century up until the late 19th century the Lunda Empire was the dominant political and military force in an area that spanned northern Angola, western Zambia, and south central Democratic Republic of the Congo. The kingdom prospered as a result of its farming, fishing and iron-smelting activities.

In 1884, European countries met in Germany to divide **CENTRAL AFRICA** and the rest of the continent among themselves. This was followed by a period of colonial rule which had a profound impact on the region socially, economically and politically. The struggle for independence ensued. The year 1960 was significant as Cameroon, the Democratic Republic of Congo, Gabon, Chad, the Central African Republic and the Republic of Congo all gained independence.

1974
THE RUMBLE IN THE JUNGLE
On 30 October 1974, the city of Kinshasa in Zaire (now the Democratic Republic of Congo) hosted what is considered one of the greatest sporting events of all time. In front of a crowd of 60,000 people and an estimated billion more watching on television worldwide, the American boxing legend Muhammad Ali faced his rival George Foreman and won. The event was significant as it not only put a spotlight on Kinshasa and the continent, but turned Muhammad Ali into a hero both for his sporting talent and his outspokenness when it comes to equality.

1971-1997
NAME CHANGES
In 1971, the then President of the Democratic Republic of Congo, Joseph Mobutu, renamed the country the Republic of Zaire and himself, Mobutu Sese Seko. The River Congo became the River Zaire. Mobutu wanted to change his country's image by renaming it, himself and many of its cities as part of a political philosophy called "authenticity" that aimed at embracing African traditions and names. The country's title was later changed back to the Democratic Republic of Congo under the leadership of Laurent Kabila in 1997.

1390–1800 AD
THE KINGDOM OF KONGO
During this time, the Kingdom of Kongo was one of the largest kingdoms in sub-Saharan Africa. It covered parts of what is now known as Angola, the Democratic Republic of Congo and the Republic of Congo. The kingdom was known for its vast creative output which ranged from intricately carved ivories to finely woven textiles.

c.1400–1800 AD
THE KINGDOM OF LUBA
At the centre of the Luba Empire was a sacred king known as a "mulopwe" whose power was enforced by regional leaders. The Luba people were renowned for their rich artistic traditions of sculptures and wood carvings. They used a Lukasa or a memory board, which was a wooden device with beads and shells, to record their history. The placement, shape, and color of the beads would serve as a memory aid for the "Mbudye," men and women who worked as historians for the Luba kings. The kingdom is located in what is now southeastern Congo.

c.1600–1910
THE KINGDOM OF KUBA
The Kingdom of Kuba, also known as the Bakuba kingdom, was founded in the early 17th century. Under the leadership of Shamba Bolongongo, the kingdom flourished trading in goods like ivory and expanding its agricultural output. Creative activities such as textile manufacturing, music and weaving were encouraged by the king. The kingdom was made up of numerous ethnic groups including the Ngeende, Kel, Bulaang, Ngoombe, and the Bushoong.

1965–PRESENT
ALL AFRICA GAMES
In July 1965, the first All-Africa Games were held in Brazzaville, Congo. Around 2,500 athletes took part. Egypt was the most successful, coming at the top of the medal table. The games are considered one of the most important sporting competitions for African athletes, who are able to compete in 22 events ranging from athletics to wrestling.

People and Cultures of Central Africa

As well as being incredibly diverse in its ethnicity, culture and languages, the region has an impressive heritage of oral traditions including folklore and mythology. Carvings, statues and handmade face masks are used to mark special occasions and individuals, and are part of the richly abundant arts and cultures of Central Africa. Like in many parts of Africa, the people in this region lead lives that are a mix of the modern and the traditional.

The Ba'Aka, Ba Mbuti and Efe

Several ethnic groups live in the Congo Basin. They are the largest group of hunter-gatherers in existence today. The Ba'Aka are one group and their familiarity with the smells and sounds of the forest mean that they have excellent animal-tracking skills. They are now at the forefront of helping to trace and protect endangered animals in the area such as western lowland gorillas. The Ba'Aka will sometimes sharpen their teeth by chiseling them with a blade. For some groups this ritual is a rite of passage to mark reaching puberty and entering adulthood, for others it is done to enhance one's beauty.

La Sape

Brazzaville is the home of a fashion movement known as "La Societe des Ambianceurs et Personnes Elegantes," which translates to "society of atmosphere setters and elegant people." Members of the group, known as "Sapeur" take great pride in their appearance. They wear shirts, ties, shoes, and suits in bright, bold colors and exciting prints. They draw inspiration for their fashion choices from the 1920s dandies, who were a group of former French colonists especially concerned with their appearance and wearing smart clothes. However, members impose their own original African twist, flair, and attitude to what they wear, to express their creativity.

The Bamileke

The Bamileke are a group who live within the Cameroon grasslands, which is a mountainous region in western Cameroon made up of many different kingdoms. The group frequently migrate and travel and so can be found all over the country. The Bamileke are known for their distinctive art, much of which was created by them for the king or ruler known as "the Fon." The beadworks, carvings, and other pieces are often produced as representations of the Fon.

The **BAMILEKE** are primarily farmers, who grow staple crops such as maize and peanuts. They also raise livestock. Women are believed to help make the soil more fruitful and so they take charge of both planting and harvesting crops.

The Wodaabe

Wodaabe means "people of the taboo." They are a group of nomadic cattle herders found in Chad, but have migrated around the Sahel for centuries. They live a relatively simple life, existing on a diet of milk, ground millet, and yoghurt, as well as some goat or sheep meat. The Woodaabe men take part in a week-long courtship ceremony known as the Gerewol. During this ceremony, men dress up and display themselves to be chosen by women as a marriage partner. In order to appear more attractive, the men will paint their faces with make-up made from clay, stones, and animal bones. They will also paint their lips black to emphasise their white teeth.

The Fang

The Fang people can be found in Cameroon, Equatorial Guinea, and Gabon. They are principally hunters, but also farmers. Their social structure is based on a clan; a group of individuals with a common ancestor. As the Fang tend to migrate, they have a custom of collecting the bones and skulls of important people who have died. They place the bones into special containers, which are then decorated with wooden sculptures. These sculptures are called "bieri" and are believed to embody the spirits of the people in the container.

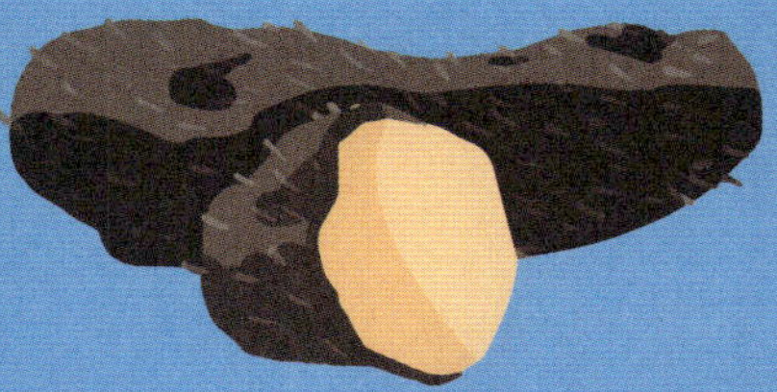

Cuisine

In Central Africa cuisine, cassava, plantains, and yams are staple foods. They are are often served alongside different stews, made from spinach or groundnuts, for example, which are regularly cooked by people in the area. Plantain is part of the banana family, but is bigger and has a thicker skin. It can't be eaten raw so is often served boiled, fried or mashed. Yams are root vegetables with tough, brown skins. The inside flesh of a yam can vary in color. Cassava is another popular root vegetable which can be cooked in many of the same ways as a potato. When ground to a powder and mixed with water, yams and cassava can be cooked into a thick dough known as fufu, which is served with soup, stew or meat. Although beef, chicken, goat, and fish are common meats, many people also eat wild game such as warthog, antelope, crocodile, and monkey.

Music

Kinshasa, the capital of the Democratic Republic of Congo has been described as "Africa's undisputed musical heart." Congolese music has traveled across borders, filling up dancefloors across the world! Drawing from a variety of musical influences, such as American jazz and Cuban music, Congolese artists have created their own catchy genres such as Congolese rumba or soukous.

WILDLIFE AND LANDSCAPES

Rainforests! Savannah highlands! Jungles! Central Africa has it all! North of Chad you can experience the blistering heat of the Sahara Desert and in the very same region find yourself navigating the cool, thick vines and towering trunks of the Congo rainforest. Central Africa is one of the greenest parts of the continent and is home to an incredible diversity of life. From the Western Lowland gorillas, chimpanzees, forest elephants, forest buffalos, leopards, giant forest hogs, and hippos, this amazing place is home to incredible array of creatures big and small.

THE MIGHTY CONGO RIVER

Zig-zagging on for 2,900 miles through nine countries in West-Central Africa is the majestic Congo River. Reaching depths of 720 feet, it is the deepest river in the world, and also a critical source of food, transport, and water to about 75 million people who live in the surrounding basin.

THE CONGO BASIN

The Congo basin is a maze of forests, rivers, swamps, and savannas which spans across six different countries. It is home to forest elephants, buffalo, mountain gorillas, and bonobos, as well as tens of thousands of tropical plants, around one thousand bird species and hundreds of fish species. Within the basin the second-largest rainforest in the world can be found, the Congo rainforest. The Congo basin is considered one of the most important wilderness areas left on earth.

CAMEROON HIGHLANDS

Along Cameroon's western border with Nigeria are a range of mountains, which include Mongo Ma Ndemi. Also known as Mount Cameroon, which means "mountain of greatness," at 13,450 feet, it is the highest point in Central and West Africa and one of Africa's most active volcanoes. The forest areas surrounding Mount Cameroon host some of the greatest biodiversity in the region, including many rare plants and animals.

THE FOREST ELEPHANT

The forest elephant can be found in the rainforests of Central Africa. They are smaller than the savanna elephant, and live in family groups of up to 20, foraging on leaves, grasses, seeds, fruit, and tree bark. Given the amount of fruit the elephants consume, they play a major role in dispersing tree species through their droppings and are sometimes referred to as the "gardener of the forest."

THE OKAPI

The okapi is often referred to as the "forest giraffe" as it is the giraffe's only living relative. With its brown coat and white stripes on its rump, the okapi looks like a cross between a zebra and a deer. It has thick oily fur that helps it stay dry in the rain. The okapi make their home in the dense Ituri Rainforest of the DRC. Similar to giraffes, the okapi has four stomachs that help them digest tough plants and animals.

THE MOUNTAIN GORILLA

One of the biggest living primates in the world is the mountain gorilla, which can be found high in the mountains of east Central Africa. They are powerful primates and can weigh up to 400 pounds! Their thick fur coats protect them from the cold temperatures high up in the mountains. For many years, mountain gorillas were threatened with extinction as a result of poaching. However, thanks to conservation efforts, the mountain gorilla population is slowly increasing.

CHANGE MAKERS AND SUPERSTARS

THE ROYAL DRUMMERS OF BURUNDI

The Royal Drummers of Burundi are considered one of the greatest percussion ensembles in the world. The group was initially created to mark various royal occasions dating back to the 16th century such as the births, enthronement, and deaths of kings. Today the drummers play at national events, festivals and concerts. Learning to play the drums is a tradition handed down from father to son. The drums are made from a local tree called the D'umuvugangoma, meaning, "the tree that makes the drums speak." The drummers are responsible for planting the seeds of the tree to ensure the drumming tradition continues.

PAPA WEMBA (1949–2016)

Papa Wemba was a Congolese musician whose vibrant and catchy tunes earned him the title of King of Congolese rumba. He was considered a mega star on the Congolese soukous and rumba music scene and helped export Congolese music to the rest of the world.

VÉNUSTE NIYONGABO (B.1973)

Vénuste Niyongabo stunned the world by taking first place and winning gold in the men's 5,000-metre race when Burundi made its first appearance at the Olympics in 1996. It was only his third time running this distance in an international competition and to this day he is Burundi's first and only Olympic gold medalist.

ALDA DO ESPIRITO SANTO (1926–2010)

Alda was the first female African author to have her work published in Portuguese. She was also a well-known figure in São Tomé and Prinicipe's fight for independence. She is the author of the lyrics of the São Tomé and Principe national anthem, and between 1980 and 1991 was a government minister, Member of Parliament, and President of the National Assembly.

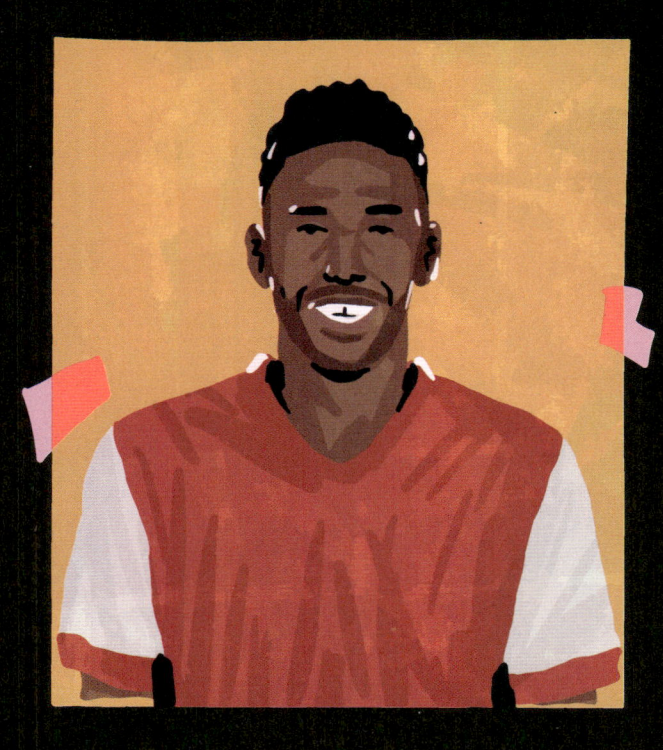

PIERRE-EMERICK AUBAMEYANG (B.1989)

Pierre-Emerick Aubameyang is the captain of the national football team of Gabon. He has played internationally for different European football clubs such as Saint-Étienne and Borussia Dortmund. He now plays for La Liga club Barcelona. He was named the African Footballer of the year in 2016.

MAHAMAT SALEH HAROUN (B.1961)

Mahamat Saleh Haroun is a Chadian film director. He is considered one of Africa's most distinguished filmmakers and his films *Bye Bye Africa, Abouna, Daratt* and *A Screaming Man* have won him numerous awards. Most of his films are based in Chad.

SNAPSHOTS

CAMEROON'S BUZZING MUSIC SCENE

Cameroon is often referred to as "Africa in miniature." This is as a result of the area's amazing geographical and cultural diversity. The country is home to over 500 linguistic groups. That richness in variety can be seen in the country's vibrant music scene. Cameroon has produced iconic musicians like the songwriter and saxophonist Manu Dibango and the multi-instrumentalist Richard Bona. The music scene is full of talented musicians who are fusing the traditional and contemporary and in doing so are creating a unique sound, such as Locko.

KINSHASA'S ROBOCOPS

Should you find yourself in the lively capital of the Democratic Republic of Congo you may well bump into Tamuke, Mwaluke, and Kisanga, three mechanic traffics cops! Standing at about 8 feet tall and weighing around 500 pounds, the robots help to control the city's busy traffic. The robots are made up of aluminum and are solar-powered. They were created by a Congolese engineer and entrepreneur Thérèse Izay Kirongozi.

GABON'S EMISSION MISSION

In 2021, Gabon became the first African country to receive payment for reducing carbon emissions by protecting its precious rainforests. The country's rainforests are vital for absorbing the globe's climate-heating emissions. Gabon has been able to show that it managed to reduce deforestation and so lower its carbon emissions in 2016 and 2017 compared to the previous decade.

SWEET SYMPHONY

Central Africa's only symphony orchestra is the Congolese Orchestre Symphonique Kimbanguiste. It is renowned for being composed almost exclusively of amateur musicians who have taught themselves how to play their instruments. When the orchestra began, 12 violinists shared five instruments, each person practising for 20 minutes before handing the instrument on to someone else. Some of the instruments were built from scratch, while others were bought second-hand. The orchestra has since gained global fame touring the world to showcase their talent and ingenuity.

DRC – THE RISE OF RELIGION

There are more Christians in Africa than on any other continent. It is estimated that by 2060 six of the countries with the top ten largest Christian populations will be in Africa. In the Democratic Republic of Congo, over 70% of the people living there go to some form of religious service every week and 90% of those follow some form of Christianity.

WEST AFRICA

West Africa is a region brimming with innovation, dynamism, and creativity. The region has a rich history of powerful empires and kingdoms. Today, the area is home to entrepreneurs, tech whizzes, scientists, artists, and innovators who are helping to shape the future of the continent.

THE GAMBIA is the smallest country on mainland Africa. It's very narrow—less than 15 to 30 miles at its widest point. Elections in this small country are unique. Gambians can vote using marbles instead of ballot papers! This system was introduced to ensure that illiterate Gambians could also vote.

CABO VERDE is an island nation consisting of ten islands and five islets. Since the 1800s, many Cabo Verdeans have traveled outside the country to find work due to drought and famine in the area. Today more Cabo Verdeans live abroad than in Cabo Verde itself.

SENEGAL Senegal is home to Fadiouth, a small car-free area made up mostly of discarded clamshells. The streets, buildings, and even the cemeteries are made of clamshells!

In 1974 **BISSAU** was added to the country's name to prevent confusion with the other West African country, Guinea. There is another African country with Guinea in its name—Equatorial Guinea.

The catchy song "Yéké Yéké" by the **GUINEAN** singer-songwriter Mory Kanté is the first African single to sell over a million copies. It was released in 1987.

One of the country's oldest and most famous landmarks can be found in **SIERRA LEONE**. It is an enormous cotton tree located in the centre of the capital city, Freetown. Believed to be hundreds of years old, freed slaves are said to have gathered under the tree as a meeting place and it has since become a symbol of freedom. Today, people come to the tree to pray or protest.

LIBERIA means "Land of the Free." The name is tied to the country's history as a home for freed African American slaves who returned to Africa.

Among the Akan, Ga, Ewe and Nzema ethnic groups in **GHANA**, children are named according to the day on which they are born. For instance, a boy born on Sunday is called Akwesi and a girl is called Akosua. These day names are usually paired with other African, religious or Western names so usually children have two names.

The name of the capital city here in **BURKINA FASO** is Ouagadougou (Wa-ga-Doo-goo). It is often shortened to Ouaga and means "land of upright people" in Mooré, the land's dominant language.

CÔTE D'IVOIRE is the biggest producer of cocoa in the world. It's likely that the origins of your favourite chocolate bar can be traced back to Côte d'Ivoire.

In 1907 the world's largest mudbrick building was built. The Great Mosque of Djenné can be found in southern **MALI** and is nearly 66 feet high and was built on a 300-foot-long platform. Every April, residents of the town of Djenné gather to help maintain the walls of the mosque during a one-day festival called Crépissage, which translates as "plastering."

NIGER has a dinosaur named after it. The Nigersaurus, which means "Niger lizard," is a 30-foot-long plant-eating dinosaur that lived roughly 110 million years ago in what is now Niger's Sahara Desert.

NIGER

NIGERIA

BENIN

Snakes are revered in **BENIN** and it is considered a sign of good fortune if a snake crosses your path. There is even a temple of pythons in the city of Ouidah that is home to more than 50 snakes.

Nollywood is the name of **NIGERIA**'s thriving film industry. It produces around 50 movies per week! It is also the country's second-largest employer, with more than a million people employed in the industry.

In **TOGO**, you will find magnificent tower-houses known as takienta. The semi-mountainous region where they are built is called Koutammakou and is home to the Batammariba people. Their tower-houses are made up of a cluster of about eight mud structures and are usually two storeys high.

POWER AND PROSPERITY

West Africa's history is filled with stories of great empires and fascinating kingdoms that rose and fell over time. Early societies such as the Nok as well as wealthy trading empires like those of Mali, Songhai, and Ghana demonstrate the richness and diversity of the continent's past. The legacy of many of these empires and kingdoms can still be seen today, in the form of art, music, and architecture.

c. 500 BC – 200 AD
NOK

One of the earliest known societies in Western Africa, the Nok, were mainly farmers and metal workers who settled near the Niger River in what is today Nigeria. They are renowned for their distinctive terracotta sculptures, some of the earliest known sculptures on the continent. The Nok were accomplished metal workers and historians have found evidence of iron tools and weapons dating back to the 4th century BC.

c. 1200 – 1800 AD
THE KINGDOM OF BENIN

The Kingdom of Benin was founded by the Edo people of Southern Nigeria. Under the leadership of Oba Ewuare, who was also known as "Ewuare the Great," the Benin Kingdom became one of the largest and most well-known empires in West Africa during his reign from 1440 to 1473. His visionary leadership resulted in a thriving capital city with a strong infrastructure. One of his long-lasting legacies is that of art and throughout his reign, Oba Euware encouraged craftsmen to create quality pieces of art. The kingdom began to lose its power during the 1800s as family members wrestled for power. Ultimately, Benin was invaded by the British in 1897, who burnt the city down and looted some rare and highly valuable treasures known as the Benin bronzes, many of which are still locked in the British Museum and are yet to be given back! The British made the kingdom part of British Nigeria up until Nigeria became independent in 1960.

1700 AD – 1900
THE KINGDOM OF DAHOMEY

The world's only all-female army originated in Benin. They were an elite trained army who contributed to the military power of the Kingdom of Dahomey. The army was made up of several thousand women and was divided into different regiments including rifle women, archers, and gunners. They called themselves N'Nonmiton, which means "our mothers." This impressive army was eventually dissolved during colonialism when the French began their expansion.

From 1967 to 1970, a bitter civil war was fought in Nigeria. The conflict was between the Nigerian government and the Igbo people, who are found mainly in the southeast of the country. The Igbos felt increasingly marginalized by the government, and wanted to establish an independent state, which they called Biafra. In the lead up to the conflict as many as 50,000 Igbos were killed. An estimated one to three million people were killed during the conflict. At its height, up to 12,000 people a day were dying from starvation.

6 MARCH 1957
A NEW DAY FOR GHANA

This date marked a momentous day in Ghana—when it became the first sub-Saharan country to gain independence! As a result, Kwame Nkrumah, the first leader of an independent Ghana became an international symbol of freedom. Other countries would later follow suit in fighting for their independence.

c.500–1500
THE KINGDOM OF IFE

Yoruba is a west African ethnic group found in Nigeria, Benin and Togo. According to Yoruba mythology, the Kingdom of Ife began when Olodumare, the Supreme Being, sent his son, Oduduwa, to create the earth. Oduduwa then became the founder and first king of the Kingdom of Ife. Ife craftsmanship can still be seen today in the form of spectacular objects made of brass, copper, bronze, ivory, ceramics, and wood.

c.1235–1600AD
THE MALI EMPIRE

The rise of the Mali Empire began in 1235 under the leadership of Sundiata Keita "the Lion Prince." Sundiata was Malinke, an ethnic group primarily found in Southern Mali. At the time the Malinke kingdom, Kangaba, was part of the Ghana Empire. Sundiata united people to fight and defeat Ghana's king Sumanguru. From there Sundiata began conquering more territories and building the kingdom he called the Mali Empire. What is most notable about Sundiata was his creation of the Kouroukan Fouga or the Manden Charter. This charter provided a spoken guideline for how people should live and behave. It focused on human rights and issues such as peace, education, and the abolition of slavery. The Manden charter was not written down and so it was passed on orally from one generation to the next.

1700AD–1900
THE KINGDOM OF ASANTE

In the 17th century what we call modern day Ghana was made up of several small groups of people from the Akan community. These groups lived separately until the early 18th century when a ruler named Osei Tutu turned them into one large empire, the Asante. By promoting a shared sense of national identity and respecting and adopting the different traditions from the groups, Osei Tutu was able to create a vast and wealthy kingdom. It traded in gold, cloth, and also in slaves, and the kingdom's wealth allowed it to buy weapons from Europe. During the 19th century, the Asante fought several wars against the British, but a series of defeats eventually led to the weakening of the kingdom. Today, the position of the king, known as the Asantehene, is still widely respected although the role is now about promoting and nurturing Asante culture.

OTHER EMPIRES

Between the 10th and 18th centuries, Niger was part of several West African empires, including the Kanem-Bornu, Mali and Songhai Empires. Senegal has the distinction of having been part of several West African empires including the Kingdom of Ghana in the eighth century, the Tukulor Empire in the 19th century and the Jolof Empire from the 12th to 14th centuries.

PEOPLE AND CULTURES OF WEST AFRICA

West Africa is a region of enormous variation when it comes to cultures, languages, and people. There are over 500 indigenous languages spoken within the region, making it an area of astounding linguistic diversity and density. While you might also see similarities in the way people dress, eat and live from country to country—each place has its own unique heritage, history, and character.

THE HAUSA PEOPLE

With a population of around 78 million, both in and outside of Nigeria, including Chad, Ghana, and Côte d'Ivoire, the Hausa are one of Africa's largest ethnic groups. Within Nigeria, the Hausas primarily live in the northern part of the country. The Fulanis are another large ethnic group. Over time the two have mixed to such an extent that they are often regarded as one group and Islam is a key component of the group's ethnic identity. Since Nigeria gained independence from Britain in 1960, the Hausa and Fulani have been politically dominant.

THE DOGON PEOPLE

The Dogon people are one of the smallest ethnic groups in Africa, made up of roughly 600,000 members who live in and around the steep hills of Bandiagara in Mali. The group is believed to have originated from the West bank of the Niger River around the 10th to 13th centuries. Around 1490 they took refuge in the hills in an area close to Timbuktu, fleeing their home to avoid being conquered by Muslims and later by the French. The Dogon are most well-known for their outstanding astronomical knowledge. The Dogon also have deep philosophical beliefs which guide all aspects of their lives. Disputes are settled in an open forum and living in harmony is an important component of their beliefs.

RELIGION

Islam and Christianity are the dominant religions in West Africa. However, communities will often continue to practice their Christian or Muslim beliefs while at the same time observing traditional indigenous beliefs and practices. For example, praying for rain at the mosque and also holding a rain dance.

Jollof Rice

Jollof is a delicious dish made out of rice cooked in a flavourful sauce of tomatoes, onions, and aromatic spices. Ask who in West Africa makes the best Jollof and you are likely to get Gambians, Sierra Leoneans, Nigerian, Ghanaians, and the Senegalese all claiming theirs to be the best! The origins of the dish can be traced back to the 1300s to the ancient Wolof Empire, which was also known as the Jollof Empire, made up of modern-day Gambia, Mauritania, and Senegal. As the empire grew, people began moving around the region, taking the dish with them, and today each plate of Jollof has adopted a local twist.

Palm Wine

A bottle of palm wine is likely to be found on tables across West Africa whether you are celebrating a marriage, mourning at a funeral, or having a simple family get together. It is a popular alcoholic beverage that is made from the sap collected from a mature palm tree. To collect the sap a palm wine tapper will climb to the very top of the tree using support ropes around their waist, as the trees can be very high—on average palm trees can grow to up to 490 feet tall! Once they reach the top they insert a tube which slowly brings the sap out into a pot known as a calabash. Once the sap leaves the tree it begins fermenting and it is this process that turns it into alcohol!

Titans of Textiles

The kente cloth of Ghana, the mud cloth of Mali, the khasa strip-woven woolen textiles of the Fulani, the Adire cloth of south western Nigeria, and the akwete handwoven textile of southeastern Nigeria, the printed cottons of Guinea... This is just a short list that showcases why many consider West Africa to be the heart of African textile production! The styles of how and when the cloth is worn varies from country to country but what is true for all these areas is the astounding skills that allow for such variety. These incredible cloths also mean that special occasions like weddings in West Africa can be a rich visual feast and a stylish affair showcasing the local textiles and different clothing styles.

The **Malian Mud Cloth** also known as bògòlanfini was made by both men and women. The men would first weave the cotton cloth on narrow looms and then the women would dye it with mud that had been fermented in clay pots for up to a year. The name bògòlanfini when translated literally from the Malian language, Bambara, means "mud cloth."

WILDLIFE AND LANDSCAPES

West Africa has a wide range of landscapes from the rolling hills of Togo to the alluvial valleys of Ghana and Senegal. Within the region you can find swamps, deserts, mountains and jungles—all home to an incredible host of creatures.

MANGROVE-RICH WEST AFRICA

Along the coastlines of Guinea, Gambia, Guinea-Bissau, Sierra Leone, Liberia, and Côte d'Ivoire are coastal forests of trees known as mangroves. Mangroves are very important as they provide food and shelter to many animals in West Africa such as crocodiles, turtles, monkeys, and manatees. Nigeria and Guinea-Bissau are two of the world's most mangrove-rich countries and mangroves in West Africa represent 13% of mangrove forest cover worldwide. As well as providing critical habitat and food sources for plants and animals, the mangroves play an enormous role economically by helping maintain a thriving fishing industry.

WEST AFRICA'S LONGEST RIVER

The Niger River stretches for over 2,500 miles. It is the third longest river in Africa behind the Nile and the Congo River. Originating in the Guinea Highlands, the river passes through Mali, Niger, and Nigeria. It provides water to more than 100 million people!

HERE COMES THE HARMATTAN!

From November until March, a dry and dusty sand-filled wind sweeps West Africa from the Sahara Desert into the Gulf of Guinea. It is known as the Harmattan. The clouds of dust the Harmattan brings can make it difficult to see further than a few hundred metres. The wind can be highly disruptive, causing flight delays and making life miserable for those with respiratory illnesses. The dust storms can also block out the sun for days!

THE PYGMY HIPPO

In Côte d'Ivoire, Guinea, Liberia and Sierra Leone you might be fortunate enough to spot a pygmy hippo. This creature is much smaller than the river hippo but it can still grow to be just over 5.7 feet long and weigh over 550 pounds! They usually live in dense forest and areas close to swamps and streams. During the day they stay in the water to avoid their skin drying out. At night, they venture into the forest in search of plants and fruits to eat.

GIANT SNAIL!

One of the largest land snails, the Ghana Snail can be found in Ghana. The snail can reach up to 12 inches in length! It has both male and female organs and can produce over 12,000 eggs each year. It also has a wide-ranging and bizarre diet—it can eat everything from plants to rotting meat to concrete! The snails extract the calcium in concrete for their shells.

THE ENDANGERED ADDAX

Niger is home to the endangered addax antelope. There are fewer than 100 living addax antelopes in the world. The addax is one cool animal and is well adapted to desert climates and so rarely needs to drink. Its coat changes from brown in winter to white in summer to reflect heat to keep it cool. The addax also has flat hooves that prevent it from sinking into the sand.

NESTING TURTLES

Cabo Verde is one of the most important nesting sites for loggerhead sea turtles in the world. Hundreds of thousands loggerhead sea turtles choose the islands as the place to lay their eggs. Loggerhead turtles are named for their large heads that support their powerful jaw muscle. Sadly, many of their nesting beaches are being used for tourism development. This loss of habitat is one of the reasons why loggerhead turtles are now endangered.

CHANGE MAKERS AND SUPERSTARS

ADENIKE OLADOSU (B.1994)

Adenike is a young Nigerian climate activist who works to bring awareness on the effects of climate change on Africans, especially women and girls. She started the Fridays For Future movement in Nigeria in 2019 to draw attention to the climate emergency.

ANGÉLIQUE KIDJO (B.1960)

Angélique Kidjo is a renowned Beninese musician who has won four Grammy Awards. Angelique has a huge musical back catalogue, having completed 13 albums. Her unique sound fuses her strong vocals with West African musical elements and American R&B,

YENNENGA (C.12TH CENTURY)

A fearless warrior, Princess Yennenga is a legendary figure in Burkina Faso's history. She lived some time between the 11th and 15th centuries where she fought against enemies to defend her father's kingdom. Princess Yennenga gave birth to her son Ouedraogo, meaning "the stallion," who established the Mossi Empire (a number of powerful kingdoms in what is now Burkina Faso). Today there are several statues and roads named after Yennenga in Burkina Faso.

DIDIER YVES DROGBA TÉBILY (B.1978)

Didier is one of the most popular African footballers. Born in the Côte d'Ivoire, he was captain of the Ivorian national team and won the Footballer of the Year award twice! Didier played for Chelsea in the Premier League, retiring in 2018. Didier was equally active off the pitch speaking out about politics in his home country.

CHIMAMANDA NGOZI ADICHIE (B.1977)

Chimamanda is an award-winning and bestselling author from Nigeria. Her 2006 book, *Half of A Yellow Sun*, was turned into a film of the same title in 2013. She has since gone on to publish numerous other books, and her work has been translated into over 30 languages. Chimamanda has received numerous awards and accolades for her work, including the Women's Prize for Fiction in 2007, the MacArthur Foundation Fellowship (known as the genius grant) in 2008 and the National Book Critics Circle Award for Fiction in 2014.

THOMAS SANKARA (1949-1987)

Thomas Isidore Noel Sankara was one of the most celebrated African leaders. A charismatic revolutionary, Thomas seized power in 1983 and changed the name of his country from Upper Volta to Burkina Faso. Thomas was a politician who many felt spoke directly to the needs of his people. He prioritised education and redistributed land to the poor and led an austere life with a reduced salary. During his time in power he banned excess spending by politicians, including the use of government chauffeurs and buying first-class airline tickets. Many across Africa saw him as an inspiring leader. He was killed in a military coup four years after coming to power.

SNAPSHOTS

NIGERIA'S NEW CHAPTER

Nigeria has produced some of the world's most beloved writers. Literary legends such as Wole Soyinka and Chinua Achebe, who is sometimes referred to as "the grandfather of African literature." His book *Things Fall Apart* is still widely read today and taught in schools. There is also a new generation of writers who are making their mark. Chimamanda Ngozi Adichie is perhaps one of the best-known writers of the younger generation but there are plenty of other incredibly talented writers on the rise like Ayọ̀bámi Adébáy (*Stay With Me*), Helon Habila (*Oil on Water*), Chibundu Onuzo (*The Spider King's Daughter*), and Akwaeke Emezi (*Freshwater*).

FESPACO: AFRICA'S MOST FAMOUS FILM FESTIVAL

Burkina Faso hosts one of the biggest cultural events on the continent—the famous FESPACO film festival in Ouagadougou. Founded in 1969 it is Africa's largest film festival. For one week every two years, film enthusiasts and producers flood Burkina Faso's capital to watch dozens of newly released films. The films compete to win Stallion of Yennenga, which is the grand prize for the best film. The festival is about much more than seeing the best of African cinema—it also helps those working in the industry to make valuable connections.

THE GREAT GREEN WALL PROJECT

The Great Green Wall is an ambitious and essential project to build a 5,000-mile wall of trees stretching across the entire width of Africa. The wall will cross several countries along the Sahel from the Atlantic Ocean to the Indian Ocean. Once complete, the wall will be the largest living structure on the earth. The project is about 15% underway and is already helping to bring degraded landscapes back to life. It is seen as a solution to climate change, drought and famine.

MADE IN AFRICA

Across the continent, there is a new generation of fashion designers on the rise. In West Africa, the creations of emerging and established designers can be seen during fashion week in Dakar, Senegal, Accra, Ghana, and Lagos, Nigeria as well as in the growing number of independent fashion boutiques. Designs that showcase the unique prints, patterns and textiles of different countries—made by designers who bring their own innovative approach and backstory—have made the African fashion industry one of the most interesting and promising. Some designers to watch in West Africa include the Ivorian designer, Loza Maléombho, the Ghanaian designer Atto Tetteh, the Nigerian lawyer-turned-designer Lisa Folawiyo, and the Benin designer, Kassim Lassissi.

SOUTHERN AFRICA

Southern Africa is loosely defined as the area below the Democratic Republic of Congo. This region includes Angola, Botswana, Eswatini (formerly Swaziland), Lesotho, Malawi, Mozambique, Namibia, South Africa, Zimbabwe, and Zambia. There are 11 official languages in South Africa. It also has the unique distinction of being the only country where two Nobel Prize winners—Desmond Tutu and Nelson Mandela—have lived on the same road, Vilakazi Street in Soweto.

ANGOLA has one of the youngest populations in the world with an average age of just 16!

NAMIBIA is home to desert elephants which have adapted to the harsh conditions of the area. These elephants are taller and leaner than other species of elephants and can go without drinking for days on end. Outside of Namibia they are only found in Mali. They are endangered because of poaching and habitat loss.

BOTSWANA is one of the world's largest diamond producers. It is home to the Jwaneng mine which is considered the most valuable diamond mine in the world as it produces 11 million carats of diamonds every year!

There are 11 official languages in **SOUTH AFRICA**: Afrikaans, English, Xhosa, Ndebele, Zulu, Tswana, Swati, Sotho, Southern Sotho, Venda, and Tsonga. Many South Africans can speak two or three of these languages, but very few can speak all 11! This is because many of the languages belong to different ethnic groups who traditionally live in different parts of the country.

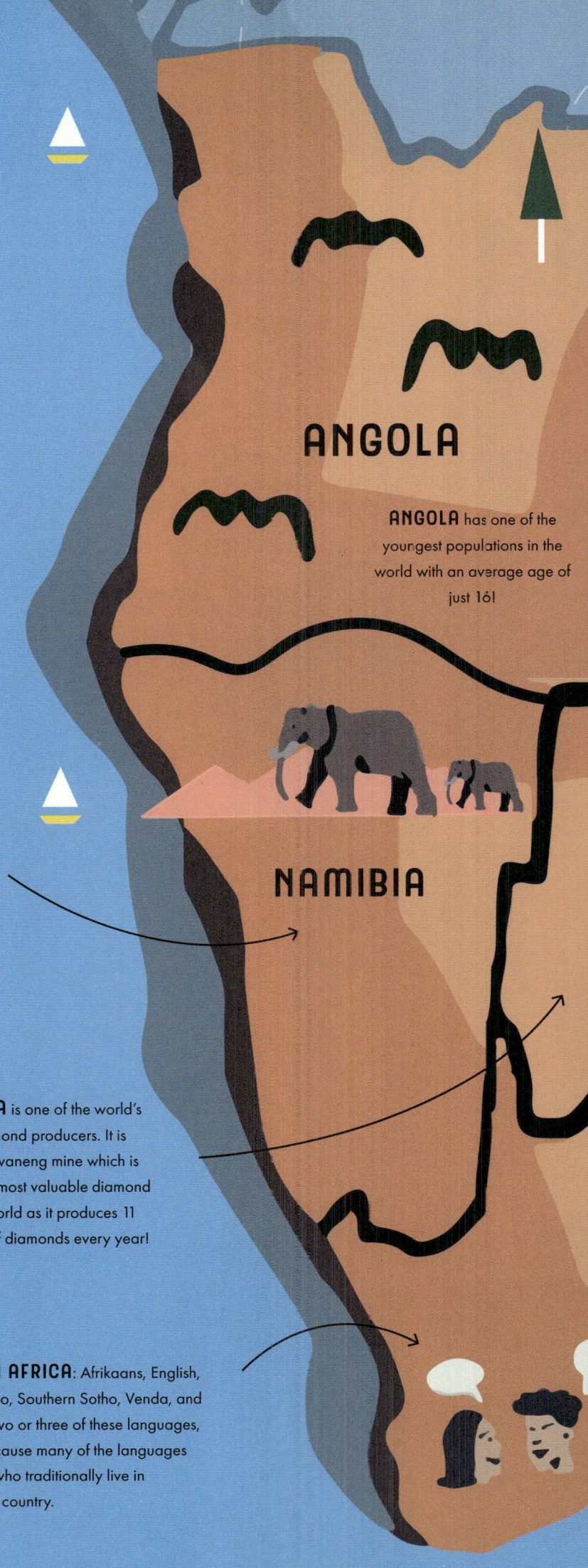

ZAMBIA shares one of the world's largest man-made lakes, Lake Kariba, with Zimbabwe.

The name **MALAWI** is said to be linked to the ancient 16th-century Maravi Kingdom in East Africa. Maravi means "fire flames."

There are more than 40 languages spoken in **MOZAMBIQUE**, which include Portuguese, Makhuwa, Tsonga, Lomwe, Changana, Nyanja, Ndau, Sena, Chwabo, and Tswa.

ZAMBIA

MALAWI

MOZAMBIQUE

ZIMBABWE

The name **ZIMBABWE** is derived from the Shona words dzimba dza mabwe meaning "house of stone."

ZIMBABWE and **ZAMBIA** are separated by one of the most spectacular waterfalls in the world, the Victoria Falls. It is known locally as Mosi-oa-Tunya or "the smoke that thunders"—and it certainly does thunder. The falling waters spills millions of litres of water per minute and can be heard up to 250 miles away!

BOTSWANA

ESWATINI

The Kingdom of **ESWATINI** was once known as Swaziland but was renamed by the ruling King Mswati III in 2018. While the name may seem new to the rest of the world, it was already referred to as Eswatini by its local population for some time.

LESOTHO

LESOTHO is one of only three countries in the world that are entirely surrounded by another country (the other two are both in Italy: Vatican City and San Marino).

The name **LESOTHO** means "Land of the Sesotho speaker." Sesotho is one of the official languages.

SOUTH AFRICA

63

GREAT EMPIRES

Southern Africa is a region full of creativity, color and unique cultural traditions—from the unique hunter-gatherer lifestyles to the foot-stomping sounds coming out of South Africa's lively music scene. The region is home to hundreds of different ethnic groups, from the Ovimbundu in Angola to the Bemba people of Zambia—each with their distinct cultural heritage which provide a unique window into the region's abundant cultural diversity.

EARLY, MIDDLE AND LATE STONE AGE

About 2.6 million years ago, in the Early Stone Age, our ancestors began using stone tools to skin and cut meat. These are known as Oldowan tools. There are two main types of stone tools—those made from flakes chopped off cores of rock, and those made from the cores of rock themselves. In the Middle Stone Age, more advanced tools were developed such as spears. In the Late Stone Age, tools for hunting such as bows and arrows were developed.

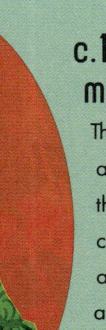

c.1300S-1600S AD
MONOMOTAPA EMPIRE

The Shona kingdom of Mutapa, ruled by the Monomutapa (or Mwene Mutapa, as it is sometimes spelt) was incredibly vast, stretching along the Zambezi and the Limpopo Rivers through sections of several modern-day southern African countries: Zimbabwe, South Africa, Lesotho, Eswatini, Mozambique, Namibia, and Botswana. The kingdom's wealth and influence came from gold trading and it flourished between the mid-15th and mid-17th centuries. However, it was weakened by war and later conquered by the Portuguese in around 1633.

The first Europeans to enter Southern Africa were the Portuguese who were looking to find a **SEA ROUTE TO INDIA**. In 1486 Portuguese explorer Bartolomeu Dias sailed around the Cape of Good Hope, which is at the southern point of Africa. Later in 1497 Vasco da Gama made the same trip. Even more Europeans such as the Dutch and British were also drawn to the Cape of Good Hope because it was a convenient stop for ships traveling from Europe to Asia.

1684-1834 AD
THE ROZVI EMPIRE

The Rozvi Empire was established by Changamire Dombo. In 1695 Dombo defeated the Portuguese who attempted to invade the empire and take control of the gold mines. In doing so, he was able to drive the Portuguese out of the area which is in present-day Zimbabwe.

1960-1990
THE INDEPENDENCE STRUGGLE

In the 1950s, many Southern African countries began to fight against colonial rule. They wanted independence and their struggle to get this was long and brutal. But slowly, over time, things began to change and between the 1960s and 1990s some African countries began to gain independence.

THE BANTU MIGRATION

The Bantu migration is considered one of the most important human movements of all time and it had a huge impact on the continent's culture, economy and politics. About 2,000-3,000 years ago, there was a massive migration of people across Africa. Bantu-speaking populations gradually left their original homeland in West-Central Africa and traveled to the eastern and southern regions of Africa. The migration lasted for 1,500 years.

The **BANTU** developed a new technology of metalwork by creating tools made of iron for agriculture.

1100-1450 AD
GREAT ZIMBABWE

Great Zimbabwe was a vast trading empire in Central Zimbabwe. Around 1100 BC, people lived in the city, which was then the capital of the Kingdom of Zimbabwe. The archaeological ruins of the kingdom are still an impressive insight into the ingenuity and creativity of the society. Later, in the 15th century, the empire went into decline.

900-1300 AD
THE KINGDOM OF MAPUNGUBWE

The Kingdom of Mapungubwe was Southern Africa's first indigenous civilisation. As communities settled on the fertile lands in the Limpopo valley between Botswana, South Africa, and Zimbabwe, the kingdom expanded, making its wealth from agriculture, gold,¡ and ivory trade. Before it collapsed in the late 14th century, it had developed into the largest kingdom in the sub-continent. Some believed that the reason it collapsed is because some of its people moved north and founded Great Zimbabwe.

1581-1663 AD
QUEEN OF NDONGO AND MATAMBA

Queen Njinga Mbandi was one of the most successful rulers at resisting European colonization during the 17th century. A military strategist and an incredible diplomat, she defied numerous Portuguese governors in what is now known as Angola and ruled the kingdoms of Ndongo and Matamba for over three decades.

1860-1960
COLONIZATION

As European settlers moved further into the centre of Southern Africa, they discovered diamonds in the 1860s and later gold in the 1880s. As a result of this, by the mid-1900s southern African countries were colonized by Britain, Germany, and Portugal.

1816-1828 AD
RISE OF THE ZULU KINGDOM

Shaka Zulu was a military leader who formed the powerful Zulu Kingdom in 1818. Zulu's kingdom was relatively small compared to some of the other communities at the time. However, as a result of Zulu's tactical mind and military organisation, the Zulus began successfully conquering neighboring peoples.

People and Cultures of Southern Africa

Across Southern Africa there are a diverse range of tribal communities whose traditions and cultural practices have been passed down over centuries. Many of the cultures in Southern Africa have a rich oral tradition with information being passed on through storytelling and word of mouth. This has meant that although stories are passed from one generation to another there were few written languages. This made recording accurate versions of the region's history difficult prior to the arrival of the Europeans, who documented their own experiences and version of events. Despite this, Southern Africa has a strong sense of identity with an incredible variety of cultures.

The Himba of Namibia

The Himba of Namibia are an ancient ethnic group of semi-nomadic pastoral people who breed cattle and goats. In Himba culture, cattle are a sign of wealth. When you die the number of cattle you owned is represented by the number of horns on your grave. Within the group, women often perform more labor-intensive tasks such as tending to the animals, building homes and carrying water, while men tend to focus on more administrative duties. Himba women are known for their distinct red-skinned look, which is created by rubbing their bodies with otjize, a mixture of butter fat and red ochre. It is believed that this mixture protects their skin from the sun and also repels insects.

The San

Kalahari's San, also known as Basarwa, are southern Africa's first inhabitants. They have lived there for at least 20,000 years and many anthropologists consider them to be the oldest human community in the world. There are an estimated 100,000 San across southern Africa, mainly in Botswana, Namibia, South Africa, and Zambia. Despite the growing pressure of modernity and mining, many San are trying to hold on to their hunter-gatherer lifestyles. San pick wild berries, herbs and roots for nourishment and medicinal purposes.

The Chewa

The Chewa are Malawi's largest ethnic group and there are an estimated 1.5 million Chewa throughout Malawi and Zambia. Central to Chewa culture is a belief that ancestors and spirits play an important part in present-day society by being in constant contact with the living world. That connection to the spiritual world is often done through the dance of those initiated to "Nyau," or secret societies.

The Xhosa

The Xhosas make up the second largest cultural group in South Africa. IsiXhosa is the language spoken and includes clicks in its dialect. For example X, Q, KR, and CG in the English language are letters that form the clicks. Xhosa traditional clothing is made from a cotton woven into unique styles and patterns. Women wear white dresses that are decorated with black binding at the hem and neck, and a headdress made up of two or three different materials of various colors. The colors of the headdresses represent the different areas they come from.

In **XHOSA CULTURE**, face painting, which is known as "umchokozo" plays a significant role. Women decorate their faces with white or yellow ochre and use dots to make patterns on their faces. The types of face painting are tied to different rites of passage.

The Shona

In Shona culture, everyone has a totem (mutupo) that represents their heritage, bloodline, origin, and identity. Someone who does not know their totem is considered "lost" because it indicates that they don't know their identity. Totems are usually animals (an elephant, a zebra, or buffalo) and are passed down through the father's lineage similar to how a surname would be passed down. Two people with the same totem would not marry.

WILDLIFE AND LANDSCAPES

Southern Africa is renowned for its stunning and varied landscapes, which includes forests, grasslands, coastal areas, and mountain ranges. The most common vegetation features of the region are savanna woodlands, dry woodlands, and grasslands. You will also find some of the continent's most iconic animals here. It is a popular destination for those looking to spot the "Big Five"—the African elephant, lion, rhino, leopard, and buffalo.

THE NOT QUITE DESERT DESERT

The Kalahari Desert is found in Southern Africa and covers more than 70% of Botswana. However, due to the Kalahari receiving more rainfall each year than most deserts, it is not considered a true desert. During the summer temperatures can reach up to 104 degrees Fahrenheit, while in winter, temperatures drop to below freezing. Within the dry savanna grasslands of the Kalahari, you will find cheetahs, lions, wild dogs, and venomous snakes like the puff adder. It is also home to a large antelope known as the gemsbok. The gemsbok has adapted to living in the Kalahari by digging for water-storing plants and roots. It also has special blood vessels in the brain that act as a cooling mechanism!

THE WORLD'S OLDEST DESERT

The Namib Desert is the world's oldest desert—it has been arid for 55 million years! The desert is as old as it is vast and stretches inland from the Atlantic Ocean. It covers large areas of Namibia along with parts of Angola and South Africa. It is home to some of the world's largest sand dunes— the Big Daddy sand dune in Sossusvlei is about 1066 feet high! Despite being extremely dry, the desert still supports a diverse number of plants and animals such as the mountain zebra and the karoo bustard bird.

THE WORLD'S LARGEST INLAND DELTA

In Botswana, you will find the swampy wetlands of the Okavango Delta. A must-see for nature lovers, the delta is one of the seven natural wonders of Africa. Its remarkable network of lagoons, rivers, islands, and swamps acts as a critical habitat and source of food for many animals, reptiles, birds, and fish.

THE BLOOMING CAPE!

The Southern Africa Cape Floral Region is one of the richest areas for plants in the world. While the Cape Floral Region covers less than 0.5% of Africa, it is home to nearly 20% of the continent's flora.

THE BIG FIVE

People travel the world over to try and catch a glimpse of the Big Five and they are probably the first creatures that spring to mind when we think of African wildlife.

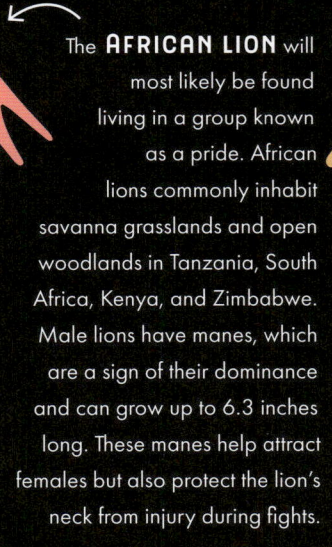

BUFFALO are considered the most dangerous of the group and are notorious for their aggressive temperament. As a result, buffalos have never been tamed or domesticated.

The **AFRICAN LION** will most likely be found living in a group known as a pride. African lions commonly inhabit savanna grasslands and open woodlands in Tanzania, South Africa, Kenya, and Zimbabwe. Male lions have manes, which are a sign of their dominance and can grow up to 6.3 inches long. These manes help attract females but also protect the lion's neck from injury during fights.

There are two types of **RHINOS** found in Southern Africa—black and white. However, despite their names both are in fact grey in color! Due to poaching and illegal hunting, most wild African rhinos are now found in just four countries: South Africa, Namibia, Zimbabwe, and Kenya.

One of the most elusive animals to spot is the **LEOPARD**. They are notoriously shy creatures and great climbers that love to spend their time in trees. Their fur acts as a camouflage, making them very difficult to spot in the wild.

ELEPHANT CALVES can be around 3 foot and 3 inches tall when they're born!

CHANGE MAKERS AND SUPERSTARS

ALBERT JOHN LUTHULI (1898–1967)

Albert John Luthuli became the first African to receive a Nobel Peace Prize in 1960. He was awarded the prize for his efforts against apartheid rule in South Africa, which separated people on the basis of race. Luthuli was a South African teacher and trade unionist who campaigned against South Africa's policy of racial segregation using a philosophy of non-violence.

MARIA MUTOLA (B.1972)

Maria de Lurdes Mutola was nicknamed the "Maputo Express" because of her unbelievable speed! During her career as a track and field runner she broke records and won numerous medals. In 1999, she completed an indoor 1,000-metre race in 2:30.94 seconds, setting a world record! At the Sydney Olympics in 2000, Maria won Mozambique's first ever gold medal in the 800-metre race and in 2008 she was added to the Africa Sports Hall of Fame.

JOYCE BANDA (B.1950)

Joyce Hilda Banda was the President of Malawi from 2012 to 2014. She was the country's first female president and the second female president in Africa. She was also a human rights activist and was named by *Forbes* magazine in 2013 as the most powerful woman in Africa. Although her political tenure was not without controversy, her appointment made history.

MIRIAM MAKEBA (1932–2008)

Zenzile Miriam Makeba was known as Mama Afrika. A talented singer and songwriter, she is credited with exporting African pop music to the rest of the world. She is perhaps best known for her catchy song "Pata Pata" which was a worldwide hit. In 1966 she won a Grammy award. As well as being a brilliant musician, Miriam also used her voice to campaign against the apartheid system in South Africa and as a result spent three decades in exile.

TSITSI DANGAREMBGA (B.1959)

Tsitsi Dangarembga is one of Zimbabwe's most acclaimed cultural figures and has published several critically acclaimed books. She is a novelist, playwright, and filmmaker, and was the first Black Zimbabwean woman to publish a novel in English. Her first novel, *Nervous Conditions*, won the prestigious Commonwealth Writers' Prize in 1989.

MPULE KWELAGOBE (B.1979)

Mpule Keneilwe Kwelagobe was the first Black African woman to win the Miss Universe title in 1999. She was only 19 at the time and was the first person from Botswana to enter the Miss Universe Pageant. She used her title to champion HIV/AIDS prevention and is now a successful model, businesswoman, and investor.

SNAPSHOTS

HERERO VICTORIANS

In Namibia, you are likely to come across a striking vision of women wearing floor-length Victorian-style gowns in vivid colors. In the early 20th century Germany occupied Namibia and during that time came into conflict with the Herero population. It resulted in one of the darkest chapters of Namibian history with nearly 80% of the Herero population being wiped out. Although the attire was initially forced on the Herero it later became a symbol of resilience. Today the layers of petticoat are worn with a headpiece made to look like cow horns.

MUSIC

South Africa is a massive music market which for decades has been exporting music to the world from Hugh Masekela to DJ Black Coffee. The lively music scene means that new styles of music are constantly emerging to fill dancefloors and airwaves. Gqom, a type of electronic dance music, and amapiano, a jazzy dance music, are recent examples.

BOTSWANA METALHEADS

Did you know that Botswana is home to an enthusiastic community of headbangers! Metalheads in Botswana use the music to speak to their lives. The country has a number of homegrown bands and they play everything from hard rock to hardcore death metal! Botswana metalheads dress in old-school biker gear—leather, chains and studs topped off with cowboy hats.

GLOBAL AFRICA

Between the 7th and 20th centuries many Africans migrated throughout the world either by force or voluntarily. Today there are more than 200 million people of African descent living outside the continent of Africa. The largest African communities are found mainly in South America, North America, Europe, the Middle East, and the Caribbean. Members of the African diaspora are very diverse in culture and appearance and they have played a major part in influencing the societies of the countries in which they live.

Forced Migration

The biggest movements of Africans happened through the Arab and Atlantic slave trades. During the Arab slave trade, Africans were taken to Europe, India, and various parts of the Arab world. During the Atlantic slave trade an estimated 12 million slaves from Central Africa and Western Africa ended up in the Caribbean and the Americas.

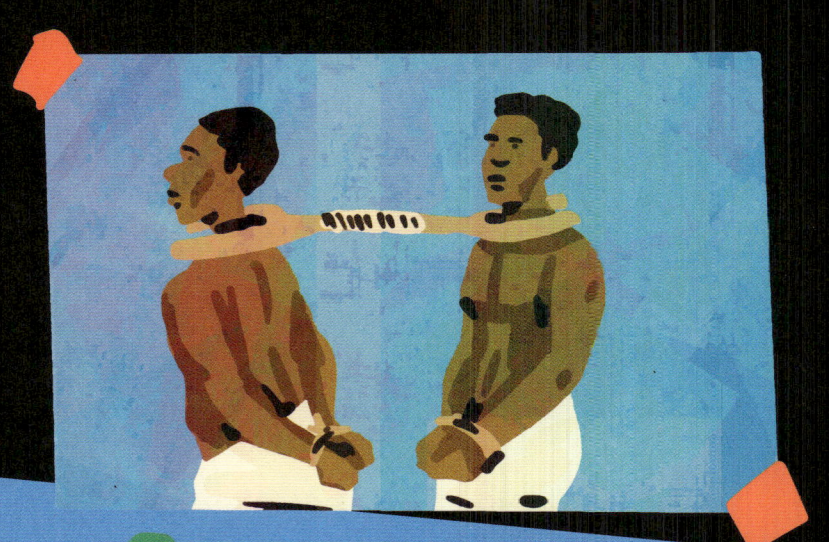

South America

Afro-Latinos are people of African origin or mixed heritage living in Central and South America. Like most of the African diaspora in the Americas, their ancestors were transported from Africa as slaves to work in mines and on plantations. The countries with the biggest African diaspora are Brazil—where nearly half of the population has African heritage—and Colombia. One of the most famous parts of Brazilian culture is Capoeira, a dance mixed with acrobatics and martial arts that was developed by African slaves in Brazil. Afro-Latino music styles, such as samba, are key components of the carnivals that are a major part of Brazilian culture, attracting tourists from all over the world.

Caribbean

Afro-Caribbeans are descendants of slaves taken from Africa during the Atlantic slave trade. In Caribbean countries such as Haiti, Jamaica, and the Dominican Republic, the African diaspora makes up the majority of the population. Afro-Caribbean culture is vibrant, distinct, and has influenced the rest of the world. Rum, a popular alcoholic drink, was invented in the Caribbean. Dances like mambo and rumba from Cuba, and calypso from Trinidad and Tobago, originated in the Caribbean. Spicy and flavourful Afro-Caribbean food is also a global favourite, including dishes like jerk chicken, goat stew, and fried plantains.

NORTH AMERICA

There are over 46 million African-Americans in the United States and they make up more than 13% of the American population. While many African-Americans trace their history to the Atlantic slave trade, the African diaspora in the United States is also made up of Africans and Caribbeans who voluntarily migrated in the 20th and 21st centuries in search of economic opportunities and a better quality of life.

African-Americans in the US lived in slavery until its abolition in 1865. Despite this, they continued to face discrimination, and fought for equal rights through the Civil Rights Movement in the 1950s and 1960s. Today, racial prejudice against African-Americans is still a major problem in American society. The struggle for equality has created many great African-American political and civil rights leaders, such as Frederick Douglass, Rosa Parks, and Martin Luther King Jnr. In 2009, Barack Obama became the first African-American President of the United States.

African-Americans have been highly influential in American culture. Music styles such as jazz, soul and hip-hop originated in African-American communities, giving the world some of the greatest musical artists, such as Duke Ellington, Aretha Franklin, Stevie Wonder, Jay Z, and Beyoncé. This is also true in many other creative industries, including literature, dance, and fashion. African-Americans have also dominated sports such as basketball, football (gridiron), and track and field. Overall, African-Americans are a tremendous source of creativity and innovation in US popular culture.

EUROPE

Between 8th century and 15th centuries North Africans, called the Moors, invaded and captured the countries now known as Spain and Portugal. An observer at the time described the Moorish invaders: "The reins of their horses were as fire, their faces black as pitch, their eyes shone like burning candles, their horses were swift as leopards and the riders fiercer than a wolf in a sheepfold at night." The Moors ruled for 800 years and the area flourished as a centre of scientific progress in mathematics, physics, and philosophy. At its height, Moorish Spain was the most modern and advanced part of Europe. Although Africans have lived in Europe for centuries, African communities began to grow during the slave trade between the 15th and 19th centuries and also in the 20th century when Africans migrated to former colonial powers such as France, England, and Belgium in search of better work and education opportunities.

MIDDLE EAST AND ASIA

During the Arab slave trade, many Africans were taken across the Indian Ocean to work as slaves and servants in Arabia, the Persian Gulf, and Asia. Descendants of these communities still exist in countries such as India, Pakistan, Sri Lanka, Iraq, Iran, Oman, and Yemen. One of the newer communities of the African diaspora is in a district known as Little Africa in Guangzhou, China. With more than 15,000 African migrants, Guangzhou is home to Asia's largest African migrant population. Many of the Africans in the area migrated there in search of business opportunities and have started businesses as traders.

HISTORY OF OUTWARD MIGRATION

All of us can trace our genetic ancestry back to Africa. About 100,000 years ago humans began migrating northwards in search of food and as a result of climate change. They crossed into Eurasia (what we know as Europe and Asia today) and over tens of thousands of years spread out to other continents such as Australia, North America and South America.

100,000 YEARS AGO

The first groups of modern humans made their way outside of Africa in what is known as the Great Exodus or the Great Migration. As a result of low sea levels and land bridges they were able to cross into other continents on foot. Over time, humans living in different parts of the world diversified into different species. Of these, only the Homo sapiens human species survives.

100 BC–700 AD

Migration continues throughout the period of the Roman Empire in North Africa as traders, merchants, soldiers, and slaves move to parts of Europe, the Middle East, and Asia.

1400–1500 AD

In the 15th and 16th centuries Spain and Portugal became the first European countries to see a large influx of Africans. Some Africans slaves are taken to Portugal to work in fishing and agriculture. Freed slaves worked in different roles, sometimes as domestic servants, bakers, or factory workers.

1500–1800 AD

The Transatlantic Slave Trade moved millions of Africans to the Americas. An estimated 12 million slaves captured from West and Central Africa were taken to Europe, the Caribbean, North America, and South America.

600–1900 AD

An estimated six million slaves are taken from East Africa and the Horn of Africa to Arabia, the Persian Gulf, and Asia as part of the Arab Slave Trade. Many of their descendants still live there today.

2010s

In the 2010s there was a significant increase in African refugees migrating to Europe and North America. Many were escaping war, violence, drought, and hunger while others were seeking a better quality of life. Unfortunately, it is common for some migrants to lose their lives trying to reach Europe through deadly routes in the Mediterranean Sea by boat.

60,000–80,000 YEARS AGO

The Great Expansion begins as humans begin to migrate in larger numbers traveling from North Africa into the Middle East and eventually spreading out through Eurasia.

45,000–50,000 YEARS AGO

Humans continue to travel, reaching Indonesia, Papua New Guinea, and Australia in simple vessels such as canoes or rafts.

15,000 YEARS AGO

The Americas are the last continents to be occupied by humans who first migrate from Northeast Asia to Alaska in North America and then travel southwards to South America over the next centuries.

30,000 YEARS AGO

Humans reached the most eastern parts of Asia such as China and Japan. Over time they replaced the indigenous population of Neanderthals living in the region, which gradually went extinct.

1960s: DECOLONISATION

With the dawn of independence, many countries celebrated being free from colonial rulers. However, some of the newly independent countries suffered from brutal wars forcing their citizens to flee to European countries such as France, the United Kingdom, Portugal, the Netherlands, and Belgium.

1980s

Africans in peaceful countries would at times voluntarily migrate to former colonial powers such as Britain, Portugal, and France in search of work and education opportunities.

2000s

Africans continue to migrate to various places around the world in search of better work, study, and business opportunities to countries such as the United Kingdom, France, and Belgium while others migrate to North America and Asia. European countries host the biggest population of migrants from Africa.

North Africans also have high levels of migration to countries outside of Africa. Africans in Algeria, Morocco, and Tunisia usually migrate to Europe which is geographically close. Africans in northeastern countries like Egypt and Sudan usually migrate to Arab countries such as Jordan, Saudi Arabia, and the United Arab Emirates.

TEN WAYS AFRICA HAS INFLUENCED THE WORLD

1. Mathematics

Multiplication, algebra, and geometry are some of the mathematical concepts developed in Africa. They can be found in Ancient Egyptian textbooks. The Ancient Egyptians were so skilled at mathematics that they used specific calculations to predict the flooding of the Nile River!

One of the oldest mathematical artefacts is the Ishango bone which is estimated to be at least 20,000 years old. It was discovered in the Democratic Republic of Congo.

2. The Calendar

The first solar calendar was created by the Ancient Egyptians. They did so by studying how the earth revolved around the sun and established a calendar consisting of 12 months and 365 days.

3. Coffee

Ethiopia is considered the birthplace of coffee. Coffee first originated in the 8th century (around 700 AD) in modern-day Ethiopia. The discovery was said to come after a goat herder named Kaldi noticed that his goats became energetic after eating red berries from a certain tree. People started to grind and boil the berries into a drink. Coffee then eventually spread north to the Arabian peninsula in the 15th century.

4. MUSIC

Many of the world's most beloved music genres such as salsa, samba, jazz, blues, and hip-hop are rooted in African influences. Samba music, which is an important part of Brazilian culture, was brought over by slaves who were influenced by African drumming rhythms. It was former slaves that also helped blues music gain popularity in the early 20th century. Today, Afrobeats, which is a musical genre from West African countries, mainly Nigeria and Ghana, is gaining increasing popularity across the world.

5. CARBON STEEL

Around 100 AD, the Haya people of what is now called Tanzania had begun making carbon steel by smelting iron in a furnace of mud and glass. This was long before modern steel making began in Europe in the 19th century. The Hayas produced high-grade carbon steel for about 2,000 years. Carbon steel is today used in cars, pipelines, railway tracks, and bridges.

6. INOCULATION

West Africans practised inoculation or vaccination before the slave trade which began in the 14th century. Africans infected themselves with smallpox brought by European settlers to immunize themselves against the disease. They would take pus from a smallpox-infected person and introduce it into a healthy person through a cut. The healthy person would experience mild symptoms of smallpox and gain immunity against the sickness.

7. PAINKILLERS

Roughly 3,500 years ago the Egyptians used the salicylic acid from willow bark to treat aches and pains before the Greeks and Romans adopted the medicine centuries later. Today the medicine is used to make aspirin, a common drug used to relieve pains and treat fevers.

8. CAT SCAN

The CAT scan was co-invented by Allan MacLeod Cormack, a South African-American physicist. In the 1960s he worked out the mathematical formula to combine the images made by an X-ray into a high-definition image.

9. DANCE

Africans have also influenced dance around the world with energetic moves and catchy beats. Dance moves such as the gwara gwara, the shaku shaku, and the poco have started dance trends on social media and have gained popularity. They are even featured in popular music videos by famous artists such as Rihanna and Beyoncé.

10. FOOD

Africa has had an enormous influence on global cuisine mainly because of slavery as well as the spread of the African diaspora. Africans introduced plantains, cassava, yams, and okra to Caribbean cuisine. They also introduced the use of hot spices such as scotch bonnet peppers in cooking. Jamaica's famous jerk chicken dish was introduced by slaves from West Africa. Southern cuisine in the United States, which includes vegetables such as collard greens and okra, was introduced by enslaved Africans.

CHANGE MAKERS AND SUPERSTARS

NELSON MANDELA
(1918–2013)

Nelson Rolihlahla Mandela is considered the father of South Africa's democracy, having served as the first Black president of South Africa from 1994 to 1999. Prior to that, Mandela was jailed for 27 years by the white minority government. When he was finally released Mandela chose to preach forgiveness and reconciliation. His dignity and courage turned him into an international hero and inspiration to many.

LUPITA NYONG'O (B.1983)

Lupita Nyong'o is a Mexican-born actress of Kenyan descent who came to the world's attention in 2014 when she won an Academy Award for best supporting actress. It was the first Oscar nomination for the 31-year-old Nyong'o, and she won it for her film debut. Lupita has gone on to showcase her diversity as an actress starring in a number of roles. She is also a bestselling author, having published a children's book called *Sulwe*.

WIZKID (B.1990)

Ayodeji Ibrahim Balogun is best-known as WizKid, the most streamed Nigerian musician in the world. His unique fusion of West African musical and lyrical elements blended with reggae, house, and hip-hop music have helped bring West Africa's Afrobeats music genre into the mainstream. WizKid's musical career started early when he was eleven and he formed a group called The Glorious Five with four friends from his church. As well as winning numerous industry awards, he regularly collaborates with other big global superstars including Beyonce and Drake.

VANESSA NAKATE
(B.1996)

When Vanessa Nakate began to notice the dramatic change in weather conditions in Uganda it led her to take action. She started a one-person campaign against climate inaction by demonstrating outside Uganda's parliament. When other youths joined her, she founded the Youth for Future Africa and the Rise Up Movement. Today, Vanessa Nakate is a leading voice among young Africans who are campaigning for action against climate change.

TREVOR NOAH (B.1984)

Trevor Noah is one of Africa's most successful comedians. Trevor grew up in South Africa under white minority rule—the child of a Black South African mother and a white Swiss father. His childhood helped shape his world view and has been a source of his best comedy material and political commentary. His colorful and at times difficult childhood is documented in his book *Born a Crime: Stories from a South African Childhood*. Trevor is now the host of a popular

SIR DAVID ADJAYE OBE (B.1966)

Considered one of the leading architects of his generation, David is known for his innovative design and creative use of materials. Born in Tanzania, David lived in various countries as a child—and during that time he was exposed to many different types of architecture. During the course of his career David has completed a diverse and impressive number of projects, from furniture design to major cultural buildings including the National Museum of African American History and Culture

WORDS OF WISDOM

Proverbs are sayings that are passed down from generation to generation as a way to advise, console, instruct, and warn individuals. They represent wisdoms that have been gained through experience over time. Proverbs are an integral part of African culture and are still widely used. Proverbs tend to come from specific communities but their provenance is not always easy to trace. The beauty of a proverb is, whether it comes from Angola or Zimbabwe, it will often contain a universal truth.

When you give a friend a goat you have to let go of the leash — **ZAMBIA**

When the threads unite, they can tie the lion — **ETHIOPIA**

Pray for a good harvest, but keep on hoeing — **TANZANIA**

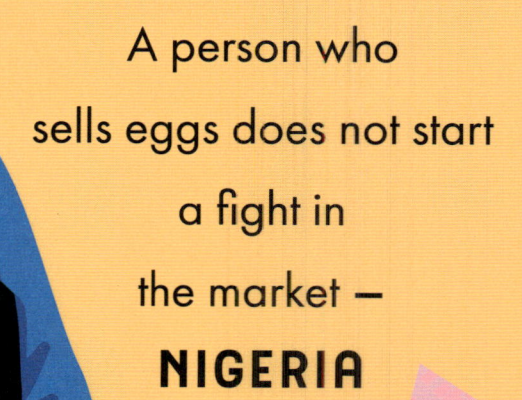

A person who sells eggs does not start a fight in the market — **NIGERIA**

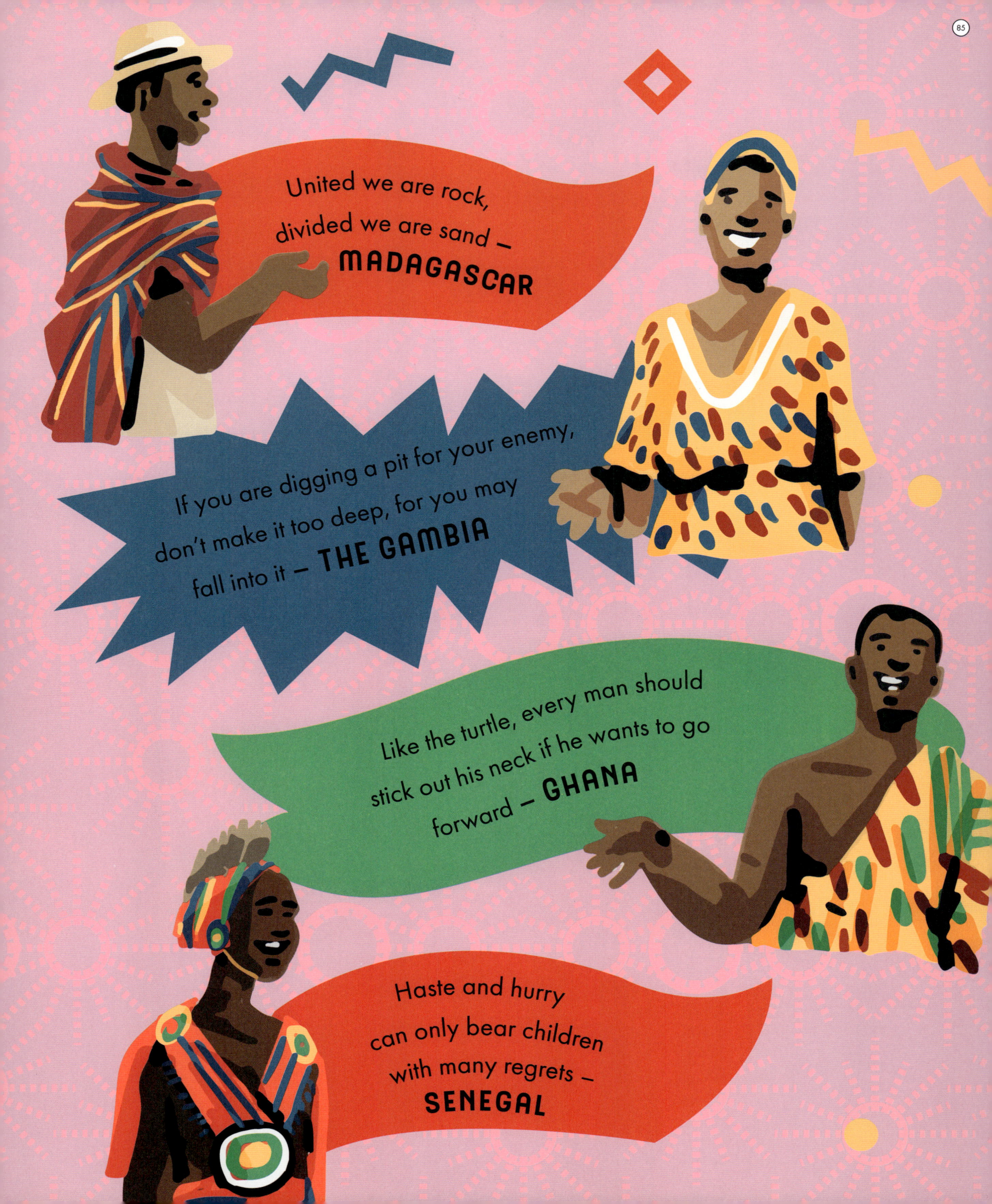

United we are rock, divided we are sand – **MADAGASCAR**

If you are digging a pit for your enemy, don't make it too deep, for you may fall into it – **THE GAMBIA**

Like the turtle, every man should stick out his neck if he wants to go forward – **GHANA**

Haste and hurry can only bear children with many regrets – **SENEGAL**

He who forgets his past is lost — **SUDAN**

The opinion of the intelligent is better than the certainty of the ignorant — **GUINEA**

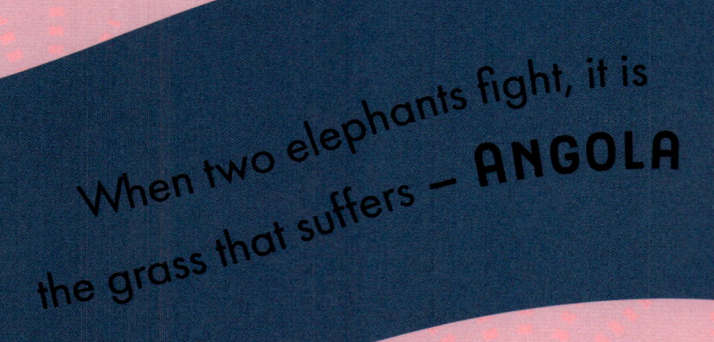

When two elephants fight, it is the grass that suffers — **ANGOLA**

He who chews two bones at the same time shall surely bite his tongue — **TOGO**

The mouth that eats should not talk, for it risks swallowing a fly — **CAMEROON**

A clean conscience makes a soft pillow — **GHANA**

You cannot lead anyone else further than you have gone yourself — **BOTSWANA**

You can never sow rice and expect to harvest maize — **SIERRA LEONE**

The tongue weighs practically nothing, yet so few people can hold it — **GHANA**

FAST FLAG FACTS

A flag can say a lot about a country. It can represent a country's past, present, and future vision. Flags across Africa share similar colors, symbols and layouts—for example many of the African flags contain the color red, yellow, and green and 25 of them feature a star.

From 1977 to 2011 the **LIBYAN FLAG** was the only plain flag in the world—it was all green with no other markings. This was to represent the political philosophy and Islamic beliefs of the leader at the time, Muammar Gaddafi. Following the departure of Gaddafi, an earlier version of the flag was re-adopted. The current flag is one that used to exist between 1951 to 1969.

The stripes on **BOTSWANA**'s flag are inspired by the country's national animal, the zebra.

The **NIGERIAN** flag was designed by a 23-year-old student, Michael Taiwo Akinkunmi, who entered a competition in 1959, a year before Nigeria's independence. The flag comprises three equal-sized vertical stripes. The green stripes represent the nation's agricultural industry and vegetation. The white stripe represents a desire for unity and peace.

To ensure that people are respectful of the **SOUTH AFRICAN** flag there are some rules that need to be observed—these include not using the flag as a tablecloth and making sure it doesn't touch the ground! The flag should also be the first to be lifted and the last to be lowered if it is being raised with other national flags.

The study of flags is known as **VEXILLOLOGY** and one of the most prominent vexillogists in Africa was Frederick Brownell who designed both the South African and the Namibian flag.

ALGERIA is one of many countries that displays a religious sign on its flag. The crescent, star, and color green are traditional symbols of the state religion—Islam.

The **LIBERIAN** flag bears a strong resemblance to the American flag—both flags have red and white stripes, white star(s), and a blue canton (square) located in the upper left corner. The resemblance is because Liberia was founded by freed slaves who wanted to represent the ideals of the United States in their flag.

The flags of Romania and **CHAD** are virtually identical. Both flags have blue, yellow, and red stripes, although experts say the blue color in Chad's flag is darker than that used in Romania's version.

MOZAMBIQUE is one of a few countries that has a weapon displayed on its flag to convey a message of vigilance and the importance of national defence following years of war. On the flag you can see an AK-47 firearm crossed with a farming hoe on top of a book. Other countries that also have firearms on their flags include Guatemala, Haiti, and Bolivia.

ALGERIA	ANGOLA	BENIN	BOTSWANA	BUR...
CHAD	COMOROS	DJIBOUTI	DR CONGO	
GABON	GAMBIA	GHANA	GUINEA	GUIN...
LIBYA	MADAGASCAR	MALAWI	MALI	M...
NIGER	NIGERIA	REPUBLIC OF THE CONGO	RWANDA	SÃO...
SOUTH AFRICA	SOUTH SUDAN	SUDAN	TANZANIA	

SO	BURUNDI	CAMEROON	CAPE VERDE	CENTRAL AFRICAN REPUBLIC
	EQUATORIAL GUINEA	ERITREA	ESWATINI	ETHIOPIA
SAU	IVORY COAST	KENYA	LESOTHO	LIBERIA
IA	MAURITIUS	MOROCCO	MOZAMBIQUE	NAMIBIA
AND	SENEGAL	SEYCHELLES	SIERRA LEONE	SOMALIA
	TUNISIA	UGANDA	ZAMBIA	ZIMBABWE

GLOSSARY

AD The official term is "Anno Domini" which is Latin for "in the year of the Lord," which refers to any years that happened after Jesus Christ.

AFTERLIFE Refers to life after death.

AIDS (Acquired Immune Deficiency Syndrome) The name used to describe a number of potentially life-threatening infections and illnesses that happen when your immune system has been severely damaged by the HIV virus.

ALTITUDE The height of an object or point in relation to sea level of ground level.

AMATEUR A person who does something for enjoyment and without professional skill.

ANCESTORS Someone a person is related to but lived a long time ago.

ANNEXED To take possession of a piece of land or a country, usually by force or without permission.

APARTHEID A policy or system in South Africa of segregation or discrimination on grounds of race.

ARCHAEOLOGICAL The scientific study of material remains e.g. tools, pottery, monuments of past human life and activities.

ARCHITECTURE The complex or carefully designed structure of something.

ARID Having little or no rain. It is too dry or barren to support vegetation.

ARTEFACTS An object, ornament, or tool that is made by a human being and is of historical or cultural interest.

ASTRONOMICAL Extremely large.

AUSTERE Without excess, luxury, or ease. To live a simple life.

BALLOT A slip of paper, carboard, or something similar on which someone marks their vote on.

BC Any years that happened before Jesus Christ came to Earth.

BEAUTIFICATION The action or process of improving the appearance of a person or place.

BIODIVERSITY Refers to the variety of life on earth.

BROKERED To arrange something such as a deal, agreement between two or more groups or countries.

CIVILIZATION The society, culture, and way of life of a particular area.

COLONIES A country or area under the full or partial political control of another country and occupied by settlers from that country.

COLONIZATION The action or process of settling among and establishing control over the native people of an area.

COMMERCIAL Making or intended to make a profit.

COMMODITY A substance or product that can be bought and sold or traded.

CONQUEST The act of taking control over a country, area or situation, normally by force.

CORRUPTION The misuse of power for private gain.

COSMETICS A set of products designed to enhance or alter one's appearance.

DANDIES A group of men who think a lot about their appearance and always dresses in smart clothes.

DEFORESTATION The cutting down of forests or groups of trees.

DEMOCRACY A system of government based on this belief in which power is held either by elected representatives or by the people themselves.

DENOMINATIONS A religious group which has slightly different beliefs from other groups within the same faith.

DESCENDANTS A person, plant, or animal that is related but lives after them.

DIASPORA A group of people with a similar heritage or homeland who have since moved out to places all over the world.

DISLOCATION A situation in which a person or thing, such as an industry or economy, is no longer working in the usual way or place.

DISPLACEMENT Someone who has been forced to leave their home especially because of war or a natural disaster.

DOMESTICATE To tame an animal and allow it to live in close contact with human beings as a pet.

DROUGHTS A very long period of low rainfall, leading to a shortage of water.

DYNAMISM Full of energy, force or power.

DYNASTY A series of rules or leaders who are all from the same family or a period when a country is ruled by them.

ECOLOGIST A person who studies the relationship between living things and their environment.

ECOSYSTEM Where a community or group of plants, animals, and other organisms that live in and interact with each other in a specific environment.

EMIGRATION The relocation or process of people leaving one country to reside in another.

ENCLAVED A country that is surrounded by another country.

ENDANGERED An creature that is close to dying out meaning that there aren't very many of that type of animal left in the world.

ENSEMBLES A group of things or people acting or taken together as a whole e.g. a group of musicians that regularly play together.

ENTREPRENEUR An individual who creates a new business.

ENVIRONMENTAL CONSERVATION The practice of protecting the natural environment by individuals, organizations and governments. Its objectives are to protect natural resources and the existing natural environment and to try and repair damage.

EXCAVATIONS The act of removing earth that is covering very old objects buried in the ground in order to discover things about the past.

FAUNA The animals of a particular region, habitat or geological period.

FERMENTING The process in which a substance breaks down into a simpler substance.

FLORA The plants of a particular region, habitat, or geological period.

FOSSILISED To preserve an animal or plant so that it becomes embedded in rock in its previous form.

FOSSILS Any preserved remains, impression, or trace of any once-living thing from a past geological age e.g. bones, shells, stones, hair etc.

GRIDIRON FOOTBALL A version of the sport names for the vertical yard lines marking the rectangular field. It's also known as North American Football or the NFL.

HIV (Human Immunodeficiency Virus) A virus that attacks the body's immune system.

HOMININ The group consisting of modern humans, extinct human species and all our immediate ancestors.

ILLITERATE Unable to read or write.

IMMUNITY To be protected and the body's immune system can fight off particular viruses, disease, or infections.

INDIGENOUS Originating or occurring naturally in a particular place.

INHABITANTS A person or animal that lives in or occupies a place.

INNOVATORS Someone or a group of people that come up with a new idea.

INOCULATION The process in which a weak form of a disease is given to a person or animal, usually by injection, as protection against that disease.

INSURANCE An agreement by which a person pays a company and the company promises to pay money if the person becomes injured or dies or to pay for the value of property lost or damaged.

INTERMITTENT Occurring at irregular intervals but not continuous or steady.

JUDICIARY SYSTEM The part of a country's government that is responsible for its legal system and has the authority to sort out arguments, disagreements, defend and apply the law of said country.

KALEIDOSCOPE A constantly changing pattern or sequence of elements.

LANDLOCKED A country that is almost or entirely surrounded by land.

LATITUDE The angular distance of a place north or south of the earth's equator.

LUCRATIVE Producing wealth or profit.

MARGINALIZED To treat a person or group of people as insignificant.

METALHEADS A fan of heavy metal music.

MIGRATION The movement of people as they leave one place to go to another.

MIZRAHI JEWS The term is used to refer to Jews of Middle Eastern and North African origin.

MUMMIFICATION The process of preserving and treating a dead body in Ancient Egypt. It usually involves removing all moisture from the body, leaving only a dried form that would not easily decay.

NEOLITHIC Relating to the later part of the Stone Age.

NOMADIC Living the life of a nomad, who is someone that travels from place to place to find fresh pasture for its animals and therefore has no permanent home.

PAN AFRICA Relating to all people of African birth or descent

PAPYRUS A material prepared in Ancient Egypt from the stem of a water plant, used in sheets throughout the ancient Mediterranean world for writing, painting, and making rope.

PARLIAMENT The group of elected politicians or other people who make the laws for their country.

PERSECUTION The hostility and ill-treatment of someone or a group people because of race, politics, or religious beliefs.

PHARAOHS A ruler in Ancient Egypt.

PICTOGRAPHS An ancient or prehistoric drawing or painting on a rock wall.

PLATEAUS An area of fairly level high ground.

POACHING The illegal hunting or capturing of wild animals.

PREINDUSTRIAL Relating to a time before countries began the process by which their economy was transformed from creating basic agricultural goods to creating and manufacturing products.

PRIMATES A member of the group of mammals which includes humans, monkeys, and apes.

PROTECTORATE A state or country that is controlled and protected by another more powerful country.

PROVERB A short traditional saying that expresses some obvious truth or familiar experience.

RADIATION The process in which energy is emitted as particles or waves.

RASTAFARIAN A religious movement among Black Jamaicans that teaches the eventual redemption of Black people and their return to Africa.

REFUGEES A person who has been forced to leave their country in order to escape war, persecution, or natural disaster.

RENAISSANCE ERA This was a period of time from the 14th to the 17th century in Europe, promoting the rediscovery of classical philosophy, literature, and art.

RESPIRATORY The act or process of breathing.

SEPHARDIC JEWS Refer to the members or descendants of Jews who were expelled from Spain and Portugal in the late 15th century.

SETSWANA The Bantu language of the Tswana people. It is one of the official languages in South Africa.

SETTLEMENT A place where people establish a community.

SMELTING To melt an ore in order to separate the metal.

SUBSPECIES a particular type within a species, the members of which are different in some clear ways from each other.

SULPHUR A pale-yellow element that occurs widely in nature, especially in volcanic deposits, minerals, natural gas etc.

SUSTAINABLE The process by which we're meeting our own needs without compromising the ability of future generations to meet their own needs.

TAILORING To make or prepare something following particular instructions.

TRADE The action of buying and selling goods and services.

UPRISING an act of speaking out, sometimes using violence, by many people in one area of a country against those who are in power

VACCINATION The act of introducing a substance into someone's body to prevent them from getting a specific disease.

VADZIMU The living-dead or ancestral spirits among the Shona people.

VEXILLOLOGY The study of the history of symbolism and flags.

VOODOO A type of religion involving magic and the worship of spirits.

WONDERS OF THE WORLD Impressive monuments created in the ancient world that were regarded in awe.

INDEX

A

Abdulmajid, Iman 35
Abyssinia 29
addax antelope 20, 57
Adichie, Chimamanda
 Ngozi 59
Adjaye, Sir David 83
Afar 6, 31
Aksum 11, 29
Algeria 8, 14, 16, 18–19, 21, 24–25, 77, 89–90
Ali, Muhammad 40
All-Africa Games 41
Almohads 17
Almoravid dynasty 16–17
Ancient Egypt 7, 10, 16, 18, 20, 78, 80
Angola 9, 39–41, 62, 64–65, 68, 84, 86, 90
apartheid 11, 70–71
Arab conquests 16, 18
Arabs/Arabian 16, 18, 22–25, 29, 74–78
architecture 13, 18, 29, 52, 83
artists 23–24, 34, 41, 43, 50, 75, 81
Asante 53
Atlas Mountains 14, 21
Aubameyang,
 Pierre-Emerick 47
authors 22–23, 35, 47, 59–60, 71, 82–83

B

Ba'Aka 42
Bamileke 42
Bamum 38
Banda, Joyce 70
Bantu 10, 40, 65
Bedouins 18
Bemba 6, 64
Benin 9, 13, 50–52, 58, 61, 90
Berbers 6, 16–19
Big Five animals 69
Botswana 9, 62, 64–66, 68–69, 71, 73, 87–88, 90
boxing 40
buffalo 44, 67–69
Buganda Kingdom 28
Burkina Faso 8, 50, 58–60, 90
Burundi 8–9, 27, 38–40, 46, 91
butterflies 39
Byanyima, Winnie 34

C

Cabo Verde 50, 57
Cairo 12, 15, 22, 25
calendar 8, 19, 26, 78
Cameroon 8–9, 38–40, 42–43, 45, 48, 86, 91
Cameroon Highlands 45
Cape Floral Region 69
Cape of Good Hope 64
carbon emissions, reducing 49
carbon steel 79
Caribbean 10, 74–76, 81
Carthage 15–17
cassava 43, 81
CAT scan 81
Central Africa 10, 38–49, 65, 74, 76
Central African Republic 8, 38–40, 91
Chad 8, 38, 40, 43–44, 47, 54, 89–90
"Chapel on Biku Hill" 27
Chewa 67
China 28–29, 75, 77
Christianity 11, 13, 19, 29–30, 49, 54
cities 6, 9–10, 15–18, 25, 27, 29, 37–38, 40, 48, 50–52, 65
civil war 52
climate activist 58, 83
climate change/emergency 58, 61, 76, 83
cocoa 39, 50
coffee 26, 37, 78
colonization 10–11, 16, 18, 40, 42, 45, 77
Congo Basin 42, 44
Congo River 9, 40, 44, 56
continent size 6, 8
copper 10–11, 40, 53
Copts 19
couscous 14
cows 39
crocodiles 20, 43, 56
cultures 6, 10, 12–13, 17–18, 27–28, 30, 42, 48, 53–54, 65–67, 74–75, 79, 84

D

Dahomey Kingdom 52
dama gazelle 20
Danakil depression 26
dance 13, 31, 54, 67, 74–75, 81
Dangarembga, Tsitsi 71
Democratic Republic of the
 Congo 9, 12, 38–41, 43, 46, 48–49, 56, 78, 90
deserts 6, 8–9, 12, 14, 16, 18–20, 25, 38, 44, 51, 56–57, 62, 68
diamonds 62, 65
Djenné 51
Djibouti 8, 15, 31, 90
Dinka 30
do Espirito Santo, Alda 47
Dogon 54
Drogba Tébily, Didier Yves 59

E

East Africa 6, 8, 10, 26–37, 63, 76
ecologist 29, 34
Egypt 7–8, 10, 15–20, 22, 25, 28–29, 41, 77–78, 80, 90
El Saadawi, Nawal 22
elephant shrew 13
elephants 7, 13, 16, 27, 31–32, 39, 44–45, 62, 67–69, 86
empires 7, 10–11, 17, 19, 28–29, 40–41, 50, 52–53, 55, 58, 64–65, 76
engineer 34
equator 38–39
Equatorial Guinea 9, 38–39, 43, 50, 91
Eritrea 8, 11, 26, 29, 31, 33, 91
Eritrea Highlands 33
Eswatini 9, 14, 62–64, 91
Ethiopia 7–8, 10–11, 13, 26–29, 31, 33–34, 36–37, 78, 84, 91
Ethiopian wolf 7, 33
"Eye of the Sahara"/'Eye of Africa" 14

F

Fadiouth 50
Fang 43
farming 17, 19, 25, 35, 40, 42–43, 52, 89
fashion designers 61
festivals 24, 46, 51, 60
films 7, 9, 47, 51, 60, 71, 82
flags 88–91
food 14, 43, 55, 81
fossils 7, 10, 29

G

Gabon 9, 38–40, 43, 47, 49, 90

Gebrselassie, Haile 35
Ge'ez alphabet 11, 29
genocide 28
Ghana 7–8, 11, 50, 52–57, 61, 79, 85, 87, 90
Ghana Empire 7, 11, 52–53
Gnawa 24
gold 11, 28–30, 53, 64–65
gold medal 30, 46
gorillas 7, 32, 42, 44–45
green energy 25
Great Green Wall 61
Great Zimbabwe 9–10, 65, 69, 84, 91
Guinea 8, 24, 50, 55–56, 86, 90
Guinea-Bissau 8, 50, 56, 90
Gurnah, Abdulrazak 35

H

Hajjaj, Hassan 23
Harmattan 56
Haroun, Mahamat Saleh 47
Hausas 54
Herero 6, 72
highlands 6–7, 11, 33, 45, 56
Himba 12, 66
hippos 16, 44, 57
Homo habilis 29
hyena 21

I

Ife Kingdom 11, 53
independence 11, 16, 27, 29, 40, 47, 52, 54, 64, 77, 88
inoculation 80
Ivory Coast 8–9, 39, 91

J

Jews 19
Jollof 55

K

Kalahari Desert 68
Kalenjin 9, 30
Katanda 39
Kenya 7, 9, 26–32, 34, 36–37, 69, 82, 91
Kidjo, Angélique 58
Kilimanjaro 27, 32
Kilwa Kisiwani 28
Kinshasa 12, 40, 43, 48
Kongo Kingdom 39, 41
Konza Technology City 37

Koutammakou 9, 51
Kuba Kingdom 41
Kush Kingdom 28
Kwelagobe, Mpule Keneilwe 71

L
La Sape 42
Lac Assal 26
Lake Chad 38
languages 6–7, 13, 18–19, 30, 38–39, 42, 50, 54, 59, 62–63, 66–67
leopards 31–32, 44, 68–69
Lesotho 9, 12, 14, 62–64, 91
Liberia 8–10, 50, 56–57, 89, 91
Libya 8, 14–16, 18–19, 23, 25, 88, 90
Lingala 6
lions 27, 31–32, 68–69
Luba Kingdom 41
Lucy skeleton 33
Lunda Empire 40
Luthuli, Albert John 70

M
M-Pesa 29
Maasai 6, 31–32
Maathai, Wangari 29, 34
Madagascar 9, 27, 85, 90
Maghreb 15, 19
Mahfouz, Naguib 22
Makeba, Miriam 71
Mali 8, 11, 24, 50–56, 62, 90
Mandela, Nelson 11, 62, 82
mangroves 56
Mapungubwe 65
Matar, Hisham 23
mathematics 75, 78, 81
Matmata 15
Mau Mau 29
Mauritania 8, 11, 14, 24, 55, 90
Mediterranean 17, 21, 76
migration 10, 32, 35, 40, 45, 76–77
mobile money 29, 37
Mobutu, Joseph 40
modelling 35
Monomotapa Empire 64
moraingy 37
Morocco 8, 14, 16–19, 21, 24, 77, 91
Mozambique 9, 28, 62–64, 70, 89, 91
mud cloth 55
mummification 10, 17
music 24, 41, 43, 46, 48–50, 58, 71–73, 79, 82
Muslim 18–19, 29, 54
Mutola, Maria de Lurdes 70

N
Nakate, Vanessa 83
Namib Desert 9, 68
Namibia 9, 12, 62, 64, 66, 68–69, 72, 89, 91
New Administrative Capital 25
Niger 8, 50–51, 53, 56–57, 90
Nigeria 7, 9, 45, 50–52, 54–56, 58–61, 79, 82, 84, 88, 90
Nile River/valley 8, 15, 19–20
Niyongabo, Vénuste 46
Noah, Trevor 83
Nobel Peace Prize 29, 34, 70
Nok 52
Nollywood 7, 9, 51
nomads 12, 16, 18–19, 21, 43, 66
North Africa 6, 12, 14–25, 75, 76–77
North America 74–77
Nubian 26, 28
Nyong'o, Lupita 82

O
okapi 45
Okavango Delta 69
okra 81
Oladosu, Adenike 58
Ottoman Empire 17

P
painkillers 80
palm wine 55
Papa Wemba 46
pharaohs 10, 17
plantain 43, 74, 81
Portugal/Portuguese 10–11, 19, 47, 63–65, 75–77

R
presidents 11, 40, 47, 70, 75, 82
pyramids 8, 10, 17, 26
Rabat 24
rainforests 8, 38, 40, 44–45, 49
Republic of the Congo 9, 12, 38–41, 90
rhinos 16, 68–69
Rift Valley 28, 31–32
robots 48
Romans 16, 19, 76, 80
Royal Drummers of Burundi 46
Rozvi Empire 64
rumba 43, 46, 74
Rwanda 8–9, 26–28, 30, 32, 36, 90

S
Sahara 8, 12, 14–16, 18–21, 38, 44, 51, 56
Sahel 19, 43, 61
Salah, Mohamed 22
San 66
Sankara, Thomas 59
savannas 6, 19, 21, 39, 44–45, 68
scientists 23
sculptures 11, 41, 43, 52
Selassie, Haile 29, 34
Senegal 8, 11, 50, 53, 55–56, 61, 85, 91
Serengeti National Park 7, 32
Seven Colored Earths 33
Seychelles 9, 27, 91
Shona 6, 13, 43, 64, 67
Sierra Leone 8, 50, 55–57, 87, 91
Silicon Savannah 7, 26, 36
slavery 10, 24, 50, 53, 74–76, 79, 81, 89
snails 57
snakes 51, 68
Somalia 9, 11, 26–27, 30, 35, 91
Songhai Empire 7, 11, 52–53
soukous 43, 46
South Africa 9, 11–13, 62–72, 81–83, 88–90
South America 10, 74, 76–77
South Sudan 8, 27–28, 30, 90
Southern Africa 6, 8–10, 12, 62–73
Spain 11, 16–17, 19, 75–76
spices 28, 55, 81
sports 22, 30, 35, 40–41, 46–47, 59, 70
stone tools 64
Sudan 8, 11, 15, 19, 26–28, 77, 86, 90

T
Tanzania 8–9, 27–32, 35–37, 69, 79, 83–84, 90
textiles 10, 41, 55, 61
Togo 8–9, 51, 53, 56, 86, 90
trade 10–11, 17, 20, 26, 28–29, 41, 52–53, 64–65, 74–76, 80
Tuareg 18, 24
Tunisia 8, 14–19, 21, 25, 77, 91
turtles 57

U
Uganda 8–9, 20, 26–28, 30, 32, 34, 36, 83, 91
universities 14, 37

V
vanilla 27
Victoria Falls 9, 63
Voodoo 13

W
"Wakaliwood" 36
warrior 58
West Africa 6, 10–11, 13, 19, 40, 45, 50–61, 65, 79–82
WizKid 82
Wolof 6, 55
Wodaabe 43

X
Xhosa 6, 62, 67

Y
yams 43, 81
Yéké Yéké 50
Yennenga 58
Yoruba 6, 53

Z
Zagwe dynasty 29
Zambia 9, 40, 62–64, 67, 84, 91
Zewail, Ahmed H. 23
Zimbabwe 9–10, 13, 62–65
Zulus 65

For my book loving father—Maxwell Muzanenhamo Chakanetsa K.C.
To my little nieces; Emmanuella and Gbemisola. A.M.

A special thanks to Feliciana Nzungu for her
excellent research skills and B for everything.

Brimming with creative inspiration, how-to projects and useful information to enrich your everyday life, Quarto is a favourite destination for those pursuing their interests and passions.

Africana © 2022 Quarto Publishing plc.
Text © 2022 Kim Chakanetsa
Illustrations © 2022 Alabi Mayowa

First published in 2022 by Wide Eyed Editions, an imprint of The Quarto Group.
100 Cummings Center, Suite 265D, Beverly, MA 01915 USA.
T +1 978-282-9590 F+1 978-283-2742 www.QuartoKnows.com

The right of Kim Chakanetsa to be identified as the author and Alabi Mayowa to be identified as the illustrator of this work has been asserted by them in accordance with the Copyright, Designs and Patents Act, 1988 (United Kingdom).

All rights reserved.

No part of this publication may be reproduced, stored in a retrieval system or transmitted, in any form, or by any means, electrical, mechanical, photocopying, recording or otherwise without the prior written permission of the publisher or a licence permitting restricted copying.

A CIP record for this book is available from the Library of Congress.

ISBN 978-07112-6980-4

The illustrations were created digitally.
Set in Hipton Sans and Futura

Published by Georgia Amson-Bradshaw
Designed by Myrto Dimitrakoulia
Edited by Claire Grace
Editorial Assistant Rachel Robinson
Production by Dawn Cameron

Manufactured in Guangdong, China CC072022

9 8 7 6 5 4 3 2 1